21-Day Healing Program for Introverts, Highly Sensitive Persons, & Empaths

Manifesting Love to Attract Your Soulmate with the Law of Attraction : Generating Self-Love after Toxic Relationships & Emotional Abuse

Martha McDowell

Table of Content

CHAPTER FOUR: PERSONALITY TYPES, TRAITS, AND DISORDERS 67

CHAPTER FIVE: CHARACTERISTICS OF RELATIONSHIPS 87

CHAPTER SIX: WHAT IS SELF-LOVE & CARE

entertainment purposes only. All effort has been executed to present accurate, up to date, and reliable, complete information. No warranties of any kind are declared or implied. Readers acknowledge that the author is not engaging in the rendering of legal, financial, medical or professional advice. The content within this book has been derived from various sources. Please consult a licensed professional before attempting any techniques outlined in this book.

By reading this document, the reader agrees that under no circumstances is the author responsible for any losses, direct or indirect, which are incurred as a result of the use of information contained within this document, including, but not limited to errors, omissions, or inaccuracies.

Introduction

The Road to Recovery & Happiness

Recovery and moving on are no joke and they are not always the easiest or quickest things to achieve. This is a road map to help you get started on that path in a non-stressful way. It is a companion to my previous book: *Emotional Abuse Recovery: Healing Your Heart After Codependent and Emotionally Abusive Relationships - How to Handle Narcissists, Controlling, Manipulative, Toxic People and Take Your Life Back.*

Whether you have read that book or not, this book will both review that material and comprise a simple, customized plan (that doesn't take up all your time) to get to the heart of your concerns, get you 21 days closer to a happier you with stronger and more positive relationships, and help you find that elusive soulmate.

The Law of Attraction and How to Harness It

The Law of Attraction is stated as follows: "Like energy put out is equal to like energy taken in," and if that sounds like woo woo to you, then you are incorrect. It is based on some fundamental laws in both the physical and metaphysical world. The science that backs up the Law of Attraction is solid as well. Think of a pendulum or magnets, the strength or energy that is given off is fully dependent on how much or the kind of energy that is put in. This is true of so many things in our physical world as described by the term 'inertia,' Albert Einstein said, "Everything is energy," and the First Law of Physics states: "Energy cannot be created or controlled in a closed system," so if that is true (and it is), then energy is and has always been. If it has always been and cannot be created or destroyed, then it can only be transferred or moved. This is the fundamental truth of the Law of Attraction.

This is also true of the spiritual, mental, and the metaphysical world. Simply stated, the Law of Attraction says that if you put out positive energy or thoughts, then you will get positivity back. The Law of Attraction has been around since ancient times. It can be traced all the way back to the Buddha himself who believed in the idea of Karma, or that what you put out into the universe is what you get back. This idea has permeated most of the other major religions and philosophies in the form of the Golden Rule (spoken by both Confucius and Jesus) and in Proverbs 23:7 that reads, "As a man thinketh in his heart so is he." In our own modern day, moguls like Oprah Winfrey and Deepak Chopra have advocated and been examples of the great results it can bring. So if you exude positivity and happiness, then you will get that back, but if you put out negativity and sadness, then you will get... well, you get the idea. Many people have used the Law of Attraction to:

- Build wealth or improve their career
- Lose weight and improve mental or physical health
- Attract success with every project
- Increase confidence
- Attract love, friendship, or improve family/work relationships

From the earliest days of our lives, we are taught that the outside world or things beyond our control are totally in control of us. You may have heard the old sayings "everything happens for a reason" or "when a door closes a window opens." If so, then you have been taught that ultimately you can't control anything and that things just happen. This is so not true and an illusion I wish to shatter in this program. Through channeling your mind and energy into a state of positivity and combining that with some tools/skills to help you both produce positivity and recognize the right or wrong type of person, you can attract your soulmate. How do you do that? Well, it is a process that we will put together as we move through these pages. However, in brief you need to take an analysis of your past attitudes, learn some basics about human behavior, and learn to love and care for yourself. Once that happens, you will be able to put out positive vibes like love, ambition, and happiness. This needs to be coupled with an understanding of personality types that might overpower or cause strife with yours. By the end of the book, all of this will come together.

To lay a foundation for harnessing the Law to attract love, friendship, or a soulmate, you must understand a few key principles:

1. Make the conscious decision that you are ready to find love and you are prepared to do whatever is necessary to

receive it.

2. Make the conscious decision you are ready to make the necessary changes in order to create a connection with and to love yourself.
3. Mimic and put out the type of positivity and attitude you desire in a partner or friend.
4. Take the kind of care of yourself that you want from your partner.
5. Believe and remain positive that it will happen.

What is a Soulmate?

In the simplest terms, a soulmate is someone who is attracted to your soul or the sum of all your parts and pieces. They have a sense of the real you and respect your every need, boundary, dream, and desire. In addition, they have a similar or symbiotic personality type to yours, which makes for a harmonious bonding. Soulmates are not just for romantic relationships, but also for friends, co-workers, and family. The concept is the same for all relationship types, it is only the parameters of the actual dynamic that are different. A soulmate in your family or at work - are you nuts, Martha!? Actually, I am not. Think about a sibling that can finish your sentences, a friend that calls just as you were about to dial or text them, or a co-worker that knows your next move on a project before you make it. That sounds as harmonious as any lover-soulmate to me.

Soulmate relationships are deeply nourishing on a mental and emotional level. Your soulmate will be attracted to your personality, behaviors, and drive to be positive. Whether you are spiritual or religious or not, you have to realize that matching your traits and quirks with a person can lead to balanced and good relationship. If you have not found a stable and symbiotic relationship yet, it could be because of some very correctable reasons. Let's look at the reasons you could be missing out and then get on the track to correct them:

1. **You're not being the real you** - Have you been caught up in the cycle of pretending to be someone or something else to please a potential partner, friend, or even boss? Well, we must stop this destructive cycle of faking it to you make it, because it is not doing you any favors. Instead, falsely paring yourself with those that may have the tendency

to overpower you (because you are not a true match) will result in limitless toxicity, while being real will attract a soulmate.

2. **Attracting the wrong people** - We have all repressed emotions because we've been conditioned to be nice, polite, and welcoming to everyone. But the true boundaries, feelings, needs, and desires you have not acknowledged are accumulating throughout your life. Instead of attracting the right people with your honesty and true nature, you have been faking your way into a toxic trap. Remember that just because a person's behavior is toxic toward you, doesn't mean they are a bad person (well, some of them are). It might just mean they are not compatible with your personality. Not only does this cycle of repressed emotions block your true self, but it also puts you in position of destruction that cannot be stopped without a change in mindset. The *Law of Attraction* states that like attracts like energy. This could explain some of the angry, sad, or fearful people you keep running into, due to you suppressing your emotions and feelings.

3. **Your subconscious is distorting your world view** - Your subconscious mind was formed in the first formative years of life. Development experts have proven that our brains are in a sponge-like state during the formative years, and instead of forming our own distinct traits, we mimic and absorb those around us. As a result, the true you is mottled and has not yet been expressed

4. **You tend to repeat relationships** - You say all the time that you don't want friends, partners, and so on that do these things (insert your personal list) and tend to avoid saying what they want in another person. Because you are also not acknowledging your wants or needs, you tend to attract repeat partners. This is because you strive so hard to avoid the things you do not want that you end up with a person who introduces you to a whole new list of negatives. If you could adjust your view and judge based on wants/needs, then you could break this cycle.

5. **Too busy to analyze yourself** - Life is busy and hard. This leads to a hurried existence in which we run, or zombie walk, through life. So, a huge amount of

your life is on coast and you never really notice it is passing. It's like driving somewhere and then asking how you got there. We stop for takeout and fast food, we stop for gas, and we stop for a relationship and then choose from what is conveniently available, rather than looking and comparing. Most people operate at a minimum level of consciousness during most of their waking hours. The trouble is, that means your body and mind are on auto-pilot, endlessly repeating comfortable thoughts and familiar patterns. Until you willfully wake up and make real effort to reach for you want, this will repeat endlessly.

6. **Change your environment -** Your soulmate isn't looking for you in bars and clubs or even on dating apps, unless your passion is drinking or shallow one-word conversations. Your soulmate feels they are whole and complete and is out in the world doing productive things and indulging their passions. How about you? What contributions did you make in the world? What is your dream and purpose? Go to places or online

discussion forums where you can indulge this.

7. **Familiarity vs. harmony** - Even though you really want to step out of the box and find a soulmate, your subconscious nature wants what is *old and familiar*. At this point in your life, your ego is an old database of beliefs and programmed reactions. It is not the true you. It will go to any length to do its job and maintain its comfort level. The cure is to create a new routine and program that will seem harsh at first but then bring harmony.

No matter what your situation, please bear in mind that it is neither your fault nor should it be a source of shame. No person is perfect, and everyone loses their way from their best life and needs to find their way back. This book is designed to help you do just that by using some simple knowledge that can make the journey so much easier.

Chapter One: Let's Talk About You

Identifying Your Past Situation

I don't pretend to know the specifics of your past or why you are here, but I do know that you are seeking something more. You have recognized an area for improvement and are willing to change your way of thinking to improve it. That being said, we have all had toxic relationships or encountered toxic people in our lives and have most likely suffered some type of abuse. I do not say that lightly nor in jest, but it is a fact (as revealed by a National Domestic Violence Center) that 23% of women and 10% of men have been the victim of physical or notable mental/emotional abuse. Taking that statistic and considering a margin of error and multiples, how staggering must the numbers be on unreported or unrecognized abuse? For our purposes, let's look at the glaring signs of an abuser in relation to someone that is being abused:

- Jealousy/The fear that someone will get jealous

- Extreme possessiveness/Constant fear of not being where you are expected to be
- Being very unpredictable/Being unsure of what certain behavior means or what a partner will do
- Nasty temper/Constant, nagging fear of being hurt or making someone angry
- Being cruel to others/Staying in isolation
- Being verbally and emotionally abusive/Low self-esteem
- Acting very controlling/Unable to make decisions
- Warped view of sex/Fear or sadness about sex
- Blaming others/Taking undeserved blame
- Sabotaging a goal/Lack of motivation

If you or anyone you know is exhibiting these signs, then please encourage them or someone close to them to seek help.

The Many Faces of Abuse

Abuse comes in many different shapes, sizes,

and techniques, as do abusers. So no matter what you have been through, there is a way to get back to your whole self and attract people that will love and hold you up when needed. Though this book is titled specifically for emotional abuse, like my previous book it will deal with aspects of all types of abuse, as they all have a similar, tragic effect on your mental and emotional health, which are the cornerstones of well-being.

Read on to learn how to heal yourself from past toxic relationships and use a new sense of confidence and openness to attract only positive people. This book can help you learn to screen people of all types of relationships, including romantic, platonic, and business relationships. Yes, you can indeed attract soulmates for every aspect of your life, so let's get started. Your mates are anxious to meet you!

To understand where you are going, you must first look at where you have been (that's a famous quote - in different words, but famous nonetheless). To look at where you've been, it becomes necessary to define what has happened to you. As covered in my earlier book, there are many kinds of abusive behaviors, and these fall under some larger umbrella terms that define them. At first you might say, "Yes, I had a bad relationship with XYZ, but I wasn't abused per se." However, once reading on you might realize that some form of abuse was present in your life. If that is the case, then know that it was not your fault and it doesn't make you less of a person or less worthy of finding your soulmate.

You bought this program to move on from a past toxicity to a new set of better relationships, which means you have suffered from some form of anguish. It could have been physical abuse, a more mental/emotional abuse, or suffering as the victim of omission by way of neglect. Things like never experiencing physical affection or never having a loved one praise you or say I love you are a form of neglectful (omissive) abuse. It can affect your opinion of yourself and your present and future relationships. No matter what kind of abuse you have suffered, mild or severe, it can have a profound effect and should never be dismissed as trivial. It can have some of the following effects:

1. **Transmission of abuse and neglect -** People that are abused by any means are two times more likely to abuse someone in their life. That is why you

are taking the steps to heal and move on is so important, you are the ONE to break the cycle.

2. **Likely to be abused again** - A 2008 Australian study revealed that 73% of women and 23% of men are abused again, but it literally became part of their expected outcomes. Not that they want or invite it, but it is just that it becomes normalized to them and they just accept it. Again, you are breaking that cycle.

3. **More likely to get sick** - A 2009 study showed that those that experience continued abuse are twice as likely to suffer physical effects like migraines, respiratory ailments, cardiovascular disease, and other ailments. The theory is that the abuse takes an emotional toll, therefore normal physiological functions break down.

4. **Increased Mental Health Issues & Suicidal Tendencies** - A 2007 study showed that survivors of abuse have a substantially increased risk of issues like depression, anxiety, and OCD. In addition, they are far more likely to experience suicidal thoughts.

5. **Addiction Risk** - A 2002 study revealed

that abuse victims that do no treatment are three times more likely to seek solace in substances like alcohol, drugs, and food. Addiction and obesity are common symptoms of past or present abuse.

6. **Aggression, deviant/high-risk sexual behavior, violence, and criminal behavior** - A 1989 study showed that survivors of abuse are 20% more likely to engage in high risk sexual behavior, violence, aggression, and criminal behaviors to compensate for past trauma.

Types of Abuse

You might only be familiar with one or two types of abuse, but many types occur, exist, and can have devastating effects. They are as follows:

Physical Abuse: This is, in the loosest definition, abuse that occurs in the form of physical violence, and (please excuse the wording) it is the most obvious and transparent kind that exists. The signs are usually glaring, especially to outsiders looking in. This can go on for a long time, usually until the victim is abused to the point of physical retaliation or until outside forces intervene.

Verbal Abuse: This is abuse perpetrated on the victim using verbal or written communication. This type is usually hard to see for outsiders and can go on unchecked for years, especially if the victim has accepted the abuser's definition of themselves.

Sexual Abuse: This is unwanted sexual advances, touching, or situations in which anything of a sexual nature is done to or forced upon a person. This is also true in the case of minors under the age of consent, even if they say they consent. This is usually well hidden and typically only surfaces if the victim speaks up or another person speaks out on their behalf, such as another parent or grandparent for a child.

Emotional Abuse: This is the broadest and hardest to define as the other three types feed into this type. Any abuse, whether physical, verbal, or sexual, can contribute to emotional abuse, and it is usually an ingredient in the other types. Simply put, the breaking down of a person's self-esteem and mental stability is emotional abuse, and the lowered self-opinion allows other types of abuse to occur. It causes the "I deserve it"mentality that is shown in case after case.

Abuse by Omission: This is something that is often overlooked, but it applies to all the previous types of abuse in that it defines how the abuse was perpetrated. Abuse by omission occurs when someone close to you is aware you are being abused or hurt but chooses to do nothing. Many instances of mental or emotional abuse would fall under this heading. Some examples of abuse by omission are listed here:

1. Yelling
2. Calling you names or using passive aggressive comments
3. Constantly criticizing you and putting you down
4. Dismissing or mocking your feelings
5. Blaming you for things that are not your fault or blowing your mistakes out of proportion
6. Humiliating or belittling you in front of others
7. Ignoring you or your accomplishments
8. Using threats to control your behavior. This includes threats of self-harm, harm

to you, and harm to your loved ones and pets.

9. Acting jealous and possessive, including accusing you of infidelity
10. Preventing or discouraging contact with family, friends, colleagues, or strangers
11. Controlling your finances
12. Telling you what you can and can't do
13. Monitoring and controlling your activities or keeping tabs
14. Preventing you from seeing a doctor or therapist

Abuse by Commission: Unlike omission, this person not only knows you are being abused, but often is the abuser or at least takes part in it. This type of abuse is more easily identifiable as it encompasses all willful types of abuse. There are no gray areas of not knowing, it is blatant and not at all mistakable for anything else. Physical and sexual abuse would be examples.

Which one of these types of abuse have you been subjected to, and what steps did you take to start your recovery? The thing I hear from most people is that, in most cases, the recovery seemed almost as painful as their feelings during the cycle of abuse. The self-analyzation that recovery requires exposes the same raw feelings as the abuse itself. Instead of someone else breaking you down (and leaving you down), you and your therapist will break you down and then start the process of building you back up to the point of loving yourself with all the fervor normally reserved for others in your life. With that in mind, let's get started on that building process.

Day One: Who Are You?

For this exercise, imagine you are sitting with Julie Andrews (just go with it) and singing "Getting to Know You" from *The King & I*. Think about those lyrics and answer the questions they ask which build an accurate picture of the process of learning about oneself and others.

1. **Getting to Know You** - To understand, first you must acknowledge that you are worthy of getting to know. You have desires, needs, dreams, and boundaries that must get equal attention. Since this course is on attracting positive people, we must come at this with that in mind and start with boundaries. Boundaries are the limits you

place on how far you let people into your world or space. These can be both uniform or varied depending on the person in question, and there are NO WRONG ANSWERS. Think about the main boundaries you set for others when getting to know you, either mentally, emotionally, or physically, and list them now. Do they have to do with physical space, emotional openness, privacy in general, or a combination?

2. **Getting to Know all About You** - Now that you have your boundaries established, let's move on to needs. These can be both physical and emotional in nature and are the building blocks to what you are seeking. According to the behavioral psychologist Abraham Maslow, needs appear in the form of a pyramid, with needs such as shelter and food at the base building up to the more internal with self-esteem and actualization at the top. See the image below from our friends at Simply Psychology:

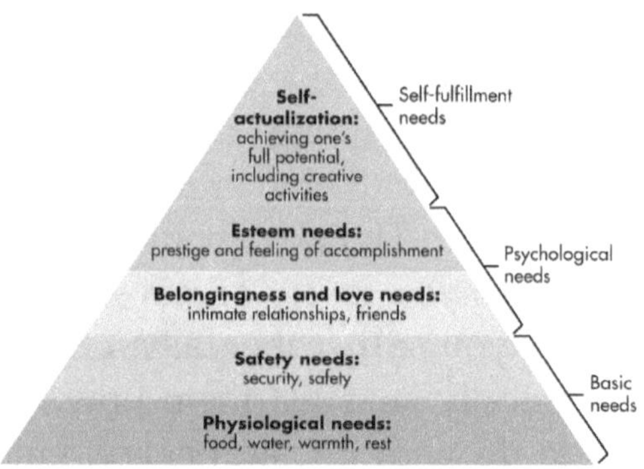

So think in those terms, place the things you need the most with future relationships (the deal breakers/things that must be met before you even proceed with one) at the base of your pyramid, then go from there to the other needs. Those things that would be ideal and "perfect" for every relationship, no matter what type. Do you have your list? Take all the time you need.

3. **Getting to Like You** - Now let's think about dreams or goals; this is the fun part! What are your dreams and aspirations? They can be as varied as your boundaries and can come from every aspect of your life, such as career, family life, entertainment or hobbies, and physical dreams, like the level of affection you

fantasize about from those in your life. Take a moment and list some of these now.

4. **Getting to Hope You Like Me** - Let's talk about your desires, which are very different things than dreams. Dreams are things that we wish for and aspire to achieve over time. Desires are things that drive you to achieve your dreams and pursue relationships. They are carnal in nature, they need to be met in both the present and the future, and they are usually not a build-over-time achievement. Like the other elements of you, they can be physical, emotional, or mental in nature. Take a moment and think of some of yours and how they motivate you in your everyday life. They should also motivate how you search for positive people to bond with in your life.

Now that we have finished with this exercise, look at your lists. Are you seeing any similarities in the four lists? Most people do. It should give you a good picture of who you are and enable you to make clear and precise decisions about who you let into your life based on their respect to the things that motivate you. Are you feeling a new confidence in your self-identity and what you want? Great, let's use that confidence and move on to Day Two.

Day Two: Narrowing Your Lists - Boundaries

If Day One was a brainstorming session, then Day Two is the polishing and refining of your brainstorming. We will take an even closer look at your boundaries, needs, dreams, and desires and help you rank them for importance. First, let's look at the list you created in Day One to identify your basic or personal boundaries. Look at the image below and create something similar to it on a piece of paper or pad.

Physical	Emotional	Mental or Intellectual

Feel free to add as many sections as needed to

list your boundaries and categorize them into physical, emotional, and mental or intellectual. To help, I am defining them below and showing some examples. You can group material and sexual under physical and time under mental. It is not an exact science, but it works for our purposes.

1. **Physical Boundaries** - These are personal boundaries that reflect simple things like the kinds of clothing you feel comfortable and confident in or more complex issues like touching or personal space when interacting with others. It even includes things as intimate as your sexual orientation. Scan your list of boundaries for things of this nature and list them under Physical.

2. **Emotional Boundaries**-These are things relating to your feelings, spirituality/religion, or deeper/subconscious connections. These are things that will dictate how much you open up to a new person or how deeply you may hide painful feelings. Scan your list for these types of boundaries and add them to that category.

3. **Mental Boundaries** - These deal with

the conscious mind and intellect and include things like education, hobbies, entertainment, and sense of humor. These are usually the boundaries that help form and drive initial conversation in the early stages of a relationship, while the previous two usually drive how deep it will become or how intimate. Scan your list for these types of boundaries and add them to that category.

4. **Sexual** - These boundaries are the sum of physical, emotional, and intellectual parts of the sex drive and sexuality. Any unwanted sexual touch, ogling from others, sexual comments, or pressure to engage in sexual acts can qualify as a destruction of a sexual boundary.

5. **Material** - These boundaries refer to personal and tangible possessions. When someone steals from you, pressures you to give or lend them your possessions, or destroys your possessions, then this boundary has been violated.

6. **Time** - These boundaries are more abstract but are very important. They deal with how you decide to use your allotment of time. People violate these

by intruding, being late, or not respecting your time. Healthy time boundaries can be implemented by setting aside time for the all aspects of your life

Now take a look at your improved/categorized lists and make a mental note of which grouping is more or less important in relationships. If they are equal, that's okay. There are no right or wrong answers here, just getting to know yourself. Are there any of them that have been universally ignored by you in the past or ones that you have allowed others to violate consistently in past relationships? Please make note of those and make sure they are made a priority going forward. This will allow for recognition of those that will consistently push your deal breakers and show a lack of respect for you. This is the first of 21 steps to narrowing the field of friends/lovers/family to those that are best for you. Here are a few tips for setting up your healthy boundary parameters.

Boundaries can seem quite difficult when we think about just how many variables we have in our life. However, the dynamics of the relationship for each is important for us to note in order to help us set our needed parameters. Being clear, concise, and non-apologetic is key. These are your boundaries and you have the right to make them as simple or as complex as necessary and to prioritize which ones take precedence. You know your body and mind better than anyone else, and it is your right to say no or yes, as you desire. Tune into your feelings, limits, and ideas of proper boundaries. This awareness will go a long way with helping you implement healthy boundaries for a happier and healthier sense of self.

Chapter Key Points:

1. Learn from your past - Review the types of abuse
2. Establish and Identify your Boundaries
3. Establish your basic Needs
4. Establish your basic Dreams
5. Establish your basic Desires

Chapter Two: Going Deeper

In Days Three, Four, and Five we will dive deeper into your sense of being by exploring your needs and desires. These will be both on the physical and emotional/mental levels which will allow you to better define the types of relationships you need and that "work for you" and the types of people to embrace or ignore. One thing I want to point out is that you should never be ashamed of any boundary, need, dream, or desire. They are all unique parts of you that deserve to be adhered to and acquired. I know you may be delving into things that are rather uncomfortable, so I wanted to make that clear from the beginning.

Day Three: Narrowing Your Lists - Needs

Today we will be performing your very own Needs Assessment (contrary to popular opinion, these are not just for businesses, they are a valuable resource in prioritizing the major things you need in all aspects of life). The definition of a Needs Assessment is an activity or process that reveals strengths, opportunities for improvement, and dominant traits. They identify the major needs of the person conducting the assessment, and the results can lead to either affirmation or modification of the needs. In simple terms, a Needs Assessment will seek to:

1. Map an improvement plan in individuals.
2. Provide an effective tool for clarifying problems and identifying effective solutions.
3. Clearly identify any problems and identify resources that can be directed towards helping to attain the need.

Take a look at your list of needs from Day One and categorize or number them from most to least important, in the sense that of some are absolute deal-breakers in terms of relationships and others have a bit more flexibility in allowing them to evolve over time (make a mental note, using the chart from Day One, on if there are more physical or emotional/mental needs). This will give you an idea on whether you are more of a physical-focused or emotional-/mental-focused person. Please remember there are no right or wrong answers here, only your answers.

Of the needs you identified, how many are deal-breakers, or needs that absolutely must be met in a relationship from the start? Those are the needs that you must prioritize when choosing whom to allow into your life in any manner more than basic human interaction. The other needs are important as well but bear in mind that there may be flexibility on those as far as needing instant or early fulfillment in human relationships, and there is room to grow into them. Just make sure whomever you choose shows a respect and understanding of all your needs.

This exercise will help you recognize people that will not respect your needs and help you avoid them and their toxicity. Also, on a happier note, it will help you concentrate on those that will meet and respect both them and you. Then you can use the improvement plan to start on a path to positivity that will exude happiness, a sense of ambition, and joy. All of those things are types of positive energy that once put out into the world will help draw equally positive people to you.

Day Four: Narrowing Your Lists - Dreams

Dreams, or goals as they can be called in our context, are those aspirations that drive you in both the daily and long-term sense. Like the other components we are talking about, they come in different packages and types.

1. **Personal Dreams** - These are what you would like to attain in your life (typically outside of work). They can be short-term or long-term in nature and are one of the major motivators of the choices we make or how we proceed in specific circumstances. These can be further be defined as either **Physical Goals** - things you wish to do to change or improve either your physical health or aesthetics - or **Mental Goals** - relating to improving your mental health or outlook.

2. **Career Dreams** - These are typically those goals relating to where you want to go to improve or change your career path.

Again using the chart from Day One (changing the categories to Physical, Mental, and Career), mentally sort your dreams into those boxes. Do you see a pattern emerging? It is fine and nothing is incorrect. This is about finding out about you, not fashioning yourself into a model you can't live with. Have you had past relationships where the other party was never pleased, or you were never "good enough?" Most of us have and it's never a pleasant situation. This will help you to stay away from those types of situations/relationships when you can and limit the issues when you cannot avoid them completely. It will help you keep on track for what you want and not for what others want for you, unless they line up with your dreams.

In addition to understanding and defining your dreams, it is a good idea to think about the Law of Attraction to achieve your dreams or goals. Here are some fundamental steps to use the Law of Attraction to reach for your dreams:

1. Dream it - Visualize your goal. Do it so well you can see, feel, and taste it.
2. Believe it will happen - Believe you will achieve it and imagine yourself after you have done just that.
3. See the plan - Make a plan to get there and visualize every step to the goal.
4. Tell it to those that matter - Tell those close to you about your dream and your plan. Talk about it and what you are currently doing to achieve it often.

5. Work the plan - Follow you plan and do progress checks. Keep going until you get there.

6. Celebrate! - You did it through the Law of Attraction, hard work, and the power of positivity

Yes, it seems simplistic, but if you don't try then you will never know. In the worst possible outcomes, you are left with positive thoughts and attitude. You have lost nothing but gained power.

Day Five: Narrowing Your Lists - Desires

DESIRES!!!!! Did you turn a bit flush or red at the term? It is ok if you did and it is a normal reaction. In today's society, we tend to get a bit flustered or embarrassed at the mention of something related to the primal nature. It conjures images of things that "just aren't done." But that's hogwash! These things are as important a part of us as anything else. They should be discussed and understood without embarrassment or chastising. That is the stance we will take in this section and book.

What are desires? In the simplest terms, they are the motivating feelings, primal urges, and wants that drive our baser instincts. Desires can dictate many things in our lives from decisions about relationships to jobs. They are normal things, so embrace them, as long as the desire is not to harm you or someone else. (If you are experiencing such desires, I urge you to seek help. There is no shame, only healing. National Suicide Prevention: Call 1-800-273-8255).

Look at the chart from Day One and modify the headings to include Physical Desires, Mental Desires, and Emotional Desires. Sort the list of desires you jotted down in our first chapter and look for your patterns. What are your main motivators? Are they lining up with the patterns from the other exercises? Whether they do or not, it's okay, and you are closer to clearer decisions about relationships.

We are not finished with your motivational snapshot, so keep your charts and notes handy as we are about to delve into how they relate to others.

Where does the Law of Attraction fit into seeking the fulfillment of your desires? Well, like everything, positivity yields positivity when seeking to fulfill any and all goals or desires. But, according to the Law of Attraction, there are some signs that you are about to fulfill your desires or needs.

1. You start noticing it or similar things everywhere - Once you change your mindset to focus on the fact you can achieve the desires of your heart, you will see signs of it everywhere. Much like you start seeing your car (that you just bought) everywhere on the road. It means your mind and psyche have started attracting the desire or goal.
2. You start noticing progress or small, mini-victories - As you progress, you will notice markers on the path to the desire as you make your way.
3. You believe and feel it happening - Just like you can sense small things as they happen, so will your mind give you cues that success is close.
4. Your mood and outlook improve - You sense success and start to get happier as the goal or desire gets closer. It is very much like a high school senior getting senioritis and excited the closer graduation gets.
5. You see and defeat obstacles - The closer

you get the more obstacles you will see, no matter how minor. But, with the positive mindset, you will sidestep them all!

Chapter Key Points:

1. Establish and Identify your Needs
2. Establish and Identify your Dreams
3. Establish and Identify your Desires
4. Categorize your Needs into Physical, Mental, and Emotional
5. Categorize your Dreams into Physical/Career, Mental, and Emotional
6. Categorize your Desires into Physical, Mental, and Emotional
7. Learn how to use the Law of Attraction to meet your Desires

Chapter Three: Defining Relationships

What exactly are relationships? Loosely defined, they are the way in which we as humans connect with other humans (and even other animals - think of your dog who is considered family). They sound rather bland and certainly not worthy of the great emphasis we humans place on them, but we know they are so much more than the state of being connected. They form the basis of our social life, which forms the basis of our existence, as we are higher primates and it is observed that the relationship unit is the building block of all primate societies. Scientists observe that even apes place a great deal of emphasis on interpersonal relationships, and it drives their societal structure, mating, and aggression. The same can be said for humans. How many times have you altered the course of your life or career to meet the needs of a family member or lover?

What we will cover in Days Six to Eight will help you identify the different types relationships and those that may be toxic in them. Though written here as relationship specific, most of these ideas can relate to all people in all aspects of life and how to screen to keep the poison to the bare minimum.

The four major types of relationships we will cover are:

1. Family
2. Casual
3. Friendship
4. Romantic

Day Six: The Family

The family is the most familiar to most people (as it is not age-specific like some of the others), because it is the first relationship we all start with and, in many cases, end with. It is the very foundation of our social education and life. These people are the ones that raise us, are raised with us, teach us, protect us, and help form many aspects of our personalities. In most cases, you do not choose this relationship, you are born or adopted into it, so dealing with toxicity within it can be necessary since you have virtually no opportunity to screen the people within it or to avoid toxic people.

The family, in regard to what we are discussing, comes in three different types (at least in the beginning, because spouse and children can come later, though spouses are covered in Romantic relationships and children are part of the unable-to-screen variety). Those types are Parents, Siblings, Children, and Extended Family.

While growing up, you are exposed to your parents and siblings with little choice about whether or not you have to interact with them, and the same goes for your own children in the future. Extended family are those members like uncles, aunts, and grandparents, where even as a child you have some choice in how much you interact with them, and this freedom expands as you get older. So dealing with a toxic extended family is a bit easier, but what about in your immediate family? Think about your own family; do you have what you would call a toxic person in it? How in the past or present have you dealt with them? What was your method, and do you still use it?

Jot down five things you have done to deal with toxicity in your family and then look at the lists we did in earlier chapters. Did you define this person as toxic (poisonous to you and your well-being) based on how they did or did not respect your boundaries, needs, dreams, and desires or because they met a definition of toxic behavior you have heard?

Signs of a Toxic Family

To help you answer this and recognize those you need to be leery of in the future, let's look at some behaviors that toxic people tend to exhibit:

1. **They have to be in control of you and everyone else** - This ranges from using money and wielding power over you to defining what you wear or meddling in decisions that you make, even as an adult. Please do not confuse normal, parental control with toxic behavior, as the main difference is the control continues in times when it is not warranted under normal circumstances. Examples would be trying to dictate anything for an independent, adult child or even micromanaging a teenager to an extreme degree.
2. **They are masters at the guilt trip and always play the victim** - You have

heard "I brought you in this world and I'll take you out" or "I raised and provided for you, so you owe me." They use the method of making you feel like you owe them to wield that control over you and keep you under their proverbial thumb. Any decision you make not in line with their wants is a slight against them.

3. **It is never their fault** - Even when they make a mistake, it is not theirs but yours or someone else's.

4. **They threaten to get their way** - They threaten you with bad actions (do what I say or I'll do XYZ to you), even if they never to it, it is their primary bargaining chip and they use it often.

5. **They are overly critical and do not consider your feelings** - Not only do they criticize any move you make, they also dismiss your thoughts on any subject and make it all about them.

6. **They favor (if the parent) one sibling over the others** - "Why can't you be like XYZ," constantly comparing you to anyone else, or giving unearned privileges to one child over another can be a sign of toxic behavior.

Is this list-making and brainstorming easier, and were you right in the assumptions you made? Toxic family members can easily violate the parts of you we have discussed and can be the worst toxicity to deal with, but remember it gets better. This is especially true with the parental family as you can start to separate from them as you get older, but what techniques can you use while caught in the fray? Let's take a look:

1. **Reinforce your established boundaries and set new ones** - In a diplomatic way, let them know what your deal-breaking issues are and ask them to respect them.
2. **Try to be as independent as possible** - Keep your grades up, get a part-time job, pay as much of your own way as you can, and be polite. This will go a long way in proving your adulthood and taking some of the threats or money issues off the table.
3. **Be attentive to signs of illness** - Has one or more of your family members changed suddenly without warning or are they showing signs of mental illness? This is not to shift the issue or make you a doctor, but just to point out that an undiagnosed illness (mental or

physical) can be the source of sudden toxic or strange behavior.

4. **Cut ties** - This is only in the most extreme cases and is reserved for those who are independent or have tried everything else.

5. **Use the Law of Attraction to try to change the dynamic** - By applying positive thoughts and actions, you might help change the situation much like "music calms the savage beast" or "you catch more flies with sugar than vinegar."

Case Study: TJ's Story

TJ is now a happy, well-adjusted, married woman, but it was not always that way. TJ was born to a 30-40-year-old couple in a small town in the Southeastern United States. The couple had been trying for years and had suffered two miscarriages in order to have a child. The couple divorced two years after TJ's birth, and she lived with her mother. Throughout TJ's childhood, her mother exhibited very controlling behavior from dressing her in frilly things (that the tom boy hated) to forcing her to enter child talent pageants and take piano lessons. Materially, TJ was spoiled, but was content with just her TV, VCR, and movies that allowed her to live in her head.

Anytime TJ would push back or express hesitation, her mother would tell her she owed her for providing for her and that it was her fault that she had to work constantly with no help from the father. She was angered when TJ established a relationship with her father, made more friends, and began becoming more independent. She told TJ many times she wished she was never born. This behavior continued until TJ joined the military at 17 (with a signature from her father) and left home. Throughout her military service and then college, her mother would offer TJ help with tuition or other things, hold it over her head as a means of control, then get angry when TJ paid her back the money.

The problem got worse as both of them aged. The mother continued to express dissatisfaction with how TJ was living her life and eventually disowned her when TJ came out as gay. TJ tried to maintain a relationship with her mother but would hang up every call or leave her childhood home feeling dejected and doubting her self-worth. Eventually, after years of trying other methods to cope, TJ cut all ties with her mother. This was not the outcome she wanted, but after so much effort, she felt it was the only way to maintain her own well-being.

This is an example of an extreme case where severing family ties is needed, but it is not needed in every case. Looking over your own notes, is becoming clearer whether a family member is toxic? How did your methods work? What would you do differently? Jot these ideas down and save them for later.

Day Seven: Casual Relationships

Outside of the family, casual relationships are the type we encounter the most (unless you are one of the lucky few with 100,000 friends, but don't brag, keep reading). These are the relationships we form with neighbors, club members, church members, children's teachers, friends' parents, and co-workers. They are not quite strangers, but not quite friends either. The great part is that if they turn out to be toxic, you can severely limit or avoid interacting with them, even in the case of teachers or co-workers, where you have outlets to address and correct their behavior if needed.

Signs of Toxic Acquaintances

How do you start to recognize possible toxic patterns in these types of relationships? Let's take a look at some common characteristics of toxic acquaintances:

1. **Version- or Personality-swapping** - Ever had that coworker you dread to see come in because you never know who they will be? One day they are bubbly and productive, the next day they are angry and gossiping. It is literally like two different people, both equally toxic.
2. **They manipulate or gaslight you** - They never seem to equally contribute to any project, but rely on guilt, sympathy, or entitlement to avoid responsibility or action and often change details of a situation to make themselves look better. There is usually one of these in every crowd, so be mindful.
3. **They project feelings** - This is that

person that projects their own feelings or emotions on to other people. Phrases like "are you mad" or "what's wrong" when you really aren't exhibiting any abnormal behavior is a red flag.

4. **They require proof of your dedication and never apologize for bad behavior** - These are the types that will require you to choose between them and someone or something else to reaffirm their own worth at the expense of yours or someone else's. If it does come to light that they are wrong, they will neither admit it or apologize.

5. **They will downplay your accomplishments and leave things unfinished** - Ever hear people say things like this, "It's great you got a new client, but they should be paying you more" or "Great you lost five pounds, but you still have so much to go." These are things toxic people say to make themselves feel better and you feel worse. Once proven wrong, they will leave a subject unfinished or never address it again.

6. **They will say toxic things in a nice way** - Or sugar-coat (as my friend in the South would say) something horrible,

like "he or she is nice" in a condescending tone about a new person or "great work as usual" sarcastically about a job you know they are not pleased with. These phrases are usually assumptive, like they already know what you are going to do before you do it.

7. **They are judgmental and over-embellish** - They will be extremely picky about things, see issues where there are none and blow up, or downplay facts to make themselves look better.

Do you know any acquaintances that act in this manner? If so, how do you deal with them and what boundaries or needs of yours did they trample? Jot these ideas down and save them for later.

Here are some tips to deal with these types of people:

1. **Enforce your boundaries** - You don't have to tell them everything about you or a project, just let them know what they need to for their job or status in your life (and that could be absolutely nothing). Remember that "silence

cannot be misquoted" (another famous quote, or at least it should be).

2. **Never be alone with them** - Keep a third party with you around them. There is safety in numbers (especially in a co-worker situation).
3. **Never overreact, and take time to cool down** – Any time a toxic person confronts you or pushes your buttons, take a moment to compose yourself before responding.
4. **Always be nice and positive** - Again, the Law of Attraction to "charm the snake."

Have you tried any of these? How did they work out? What other things can you think of to deal with a toxic casual relationship?

Day Eight: Friendships

Friends can make life more enjoyable, but they can also confuse and challenge us, so we might wonder why we bother. But without friends, life would be dull indeed, so making sure you have the right ones around you is vital. The friends we meet and have through various stages of life are important and can be very different.

The friends we meet in childhood teach us how to get along and do unto others, while those in high school are more about taking responsibility, how to have a good time, finding a career/college path, and seeking out role models. By the time we get to our college years, we find a tribe based on mutual interests and traits, and in the post-college years the focus turns to career and possible relationships, marriage, and parenthood. In all these instances, our friends are the touchstone we use to gauge our status. By the time we hit our 40's and 50's, we learn to navigate the changing tides of life, and our friends provide support and advice for new experiences. Then into our 60's and 70's, health issues inevitably arise, a friend dies, and our other friends serve as the ultimate support system.

Friendship makes the world go around and can be the most important type of relationships in a person's life. You have probably heard the old adage "friendships last longer than most marriages" and it could be true in that recent statistics place the divorce rate in the USA at 60%, a staggering number. A study from Harvard in 2008 concluded that strong friendships strengthen both cognition (conscious thought) and mental health as a person ages. Therefore, learning how to recognize toxic friends before the you let them in can be an extremely important task. Some negative traits to watch out for in regard to friendship are as follows:

1. **They make you think less of yourself** - They are the stereotypical "Debbie Downer" and seem to reflect bad feelings or perceptions on you and minimize your self-worth.

2. **You simply don't like being around them** - Do not discount the basic feeling of just not liking someone, it can be a sure sign of a person who is toxic to you.

3. **They gossip about you and you know it** - Though pretty self-explanatory, the fact you know they talk about you behind your back is a huge red flag and can't be ignored. Hey, we all like to spill the tea, but a friend is someone with whom you can share that, not someone who sloshes yours all over the place.

4. **They are a "Frenemy"** - So basically you have a love and hate relationship with them. You are friendly in a superficial

or surface kind of way, but you delight in competing and tearing at each other. That is toxic and can make you a toxic person, so beware.

5. **You can't take them anywhere** - Their behavior, no matter if socially acceptable, is embarrassing to you. That is a sign you just don't jive and the relationship is subpar.

6. **You have forgotten why you liked them** - If you can't remember why you started associating with them, then that is a pretty clear sign that you shouldn't continue.

Can you think of any toxic friendships in your past or present? Write down some examples and how you dealt with them. Compare them to the ideas below, bear in mind a true friend is not a toxic friend, so severing ties is the prime suggestion. But, if you through your selfless nature choose to remain acquainted with them, then move them from friend to casual acquaintance by using some of the following techniques, then use the ones in Day Seven once you have made the transition.

1. **Do not gossip, limit personal information** - Keep drama to a minimum by avoiding gossip about

them and keeping them in the dark about personal information.

2. **Keep positive friends around you and them** - Limit alone time with the "Frenemy" by keeping it in groups, preferably with non-toxic and true friends.
3. **Keep conversation at a shallow level** - Keep conversation light and don't delve into deep waters with them.

Have you used any of the above methods? Do you think some of them might work for your current situations?

Day Nine: Defining Romantic Relationships

Romance is the spice of life and the most profound relationship type we as social beings seek. It is probably the type of soulmate that 80% of you are seeking. Humans are one of a handful of species that mate or couple, (in theory) for life. It is often the beginning of the family unit and the end (when a child leaves the family to marry, or couple). It has become associated with the term "soulmate" as it is the ultimate goal of most people during their lives.

Though you can have many different types of soulmates, a romantic soulmate is often the most important. Let's explore what a Romantic Relationship means. Simple stated, it is a consenting relationship with mutual love and is often sexual, but not exclusively. Asexuals (people with no or little sexual attraction/drive), people who practice abstinence prior to marriage, and even those who practice celibacy as a life choice can be just as romantically connected as those who are sexually active.

As long as there is mutual love, affection, respect, and agreement on terms, then it is a romantic relationship. They have always come in many different types, but only in recent years have some types actually surfaced into the mainstream. Some of those types are:

1. **Homosexual** - Persons of the same sex.
2. **Bisexual/Pansexual**- Involving persons attracted to both sexes or those that don't place an important on sexual identity.
3. **Swingers** - Couples of any sex that practice agreed-upon sexual relations with people outside the relationship.
4. **Polyamorous** - Couples who welcome others into the relationship as equal or

limited partners based on agreed-upon terms.

All of these types are just as valid as the traditional Heterosexual type, so no matter where you fall on the spectrum, you are as real as any. Think about your current or past relationships and list the good parts of them. Now think about any possible toxicity you have encountered in the past; how did you deal with it? Make a list of those steps you took while we look at toxic behavior within romantic relationships. Please remember even the best relationships can have short periods of toxicity coming from one or more partners. The key is consistent, long-term, toxic behavior.

1. **Putting you Down** - Does your partner belittle your ideas, looks, or activities, while ignoring their own shortcomings? These are the signs of a person who wishes to control you and your opinion of yourself.
2. **The Anger Ball** - This person lashes out or overreacts about minor things. Their temper can be very scary and causes a constant fear.
3. **Guilter** - Like a toxic parent, a romantic partner can make you feel guilty or like

you owe them. This could range from loyalty to sex, but anytime guilt is used to control or manipulate another, it is toxic.

4. **Codependency** - A partner that builds their entire existence around another person is co-dependent. Regardless of whether they are cruel as a result, it is still an acid than can eat at the relationship's foundation.
5. **They Use You** - Whether it is for money or sex, no one has the right to take without equally giving back or contributing.

I hope this lesson has opened your eyes to subtle hints and is making toxic people more recognizable. Building on this, in the next chapters we will look at dangerous personality types to avoid and how to recognize and attract positive people going forward.

Chapter Key Points:

1. Identify the four major types of relationship
2. Define the Family & Recognize Toxicity within it

3. Define Casual Relationships & Recognize Toxicity within it
4. Define Friendship & Recognize Toxicity within it
5. Define Romantic Relationship & Recognize Toxicity within it

Chapter Four: Personality Types, Traits, and Disorders

In this chapter and in Days Ten, Eleven, and Twelve we will look in-depth at the most common personality types, traits, and disorders. Our goal is to help you determine how they would relate to your personality and what you would be able to tolerate in a close relationship. This will give you the skills to discern who is the best fit for you and who to avoid in creating relationships.

First, let's loosely define personality: it is the characteristics and traits that define a person and influence their behavior. That sounds very cut and dry, but we know it's so much more complex than that. By learning about personalities and the traits they have, that can help you make educated decisions about the people with whom you associate and forge bonds. In addition, behavioral scientists have defined several personality disorder types that are prone to antisocial and unusual behavior and can translate into toxic traits. We will look at all of this information and learn how to use it for your benefit.

Day Ten: Personality Types & Traits

Personality Types

Okay, I am going to be honest with you, there are sixteen defined personality types. But don't be worried, as I plan to present them in the simplest terms and in the briefest way possible. First, let us define what a personality type is: it is the sum of the traits and characteristics you possess that define your behavior. They are basically large groupings of learning or perception styles (how you take in information) that have been characterized as a type by the Myers Briggs Assessment, which took the definitions and criteria from Dr. Carl Jung (one of the fathers of modern psychology theory). Dr. Jung broke with Sigmund Freud by denying the primary role of infantile sexuality (the "Oedipus Complex" or "Penis Envy") as the basis for human personality. Instead, Dr. Jung weighted the influence of the subconscious on human personality. He attributed much of the personality to the natural traits present in the subconscious, mixed with childhood experience and future aspirations. So in his view, though initially we are subject to nature/nurture, we can change certain traits and alter our personalities to an extent. He also said that every person has four distinct ways of learning or taking in information that shape how we behave.

The test took Jung's theories on environmental perception and basic learning styles and came up with a list of styles that define their personality types. This leads to a reasonable estimation or prediction of how a person will behave or function as a whole. Each of the learning styles are represented by the first letter of its name and the personality types are named for the collective sum of the styles. The type is the combination of certain learning styles, and every theorist names them differently. For the sake of brevity and your ability to digest all of this information, I am listing the major learning styles and their overview below:

Extraversion/Introversion

Extraverted types learn best by talking and interacting with others. Those of this style prefer larger gatherings and a huge amount of varied information.

Introverted types prefer quiet reflection and

privacy. The prefer to be alone or in very small groups, with a smaller amount of information.

Sensing/Intuition

Sensing types are good at concrete and tangible things. They are logical thinkers and prefer hard facts.

Intuitive types are good at abstract things and ideas. They think with ideals and can deal in theory and hyperbole.

Thinking/Feeling

Thinking types desire objective truth and logical principles and are natural at deductive reasoning.

Feeling types place an emphasis on issues and causes that can be personalized while they consider other people's motives.

Judging/Perceiving

Judging types tend to have a structured way or theory to approach the world and judge it based on that theory.

Perceiving types tend to be unstructured and keep their options open. They believe in a gray area.

Here is quick overview of the learning styles that make up the larger personality types, with names for the combination of styles. Notice how the names they were given correlate with their major learning styles and are a predictor of the dominant behavior.

1. **Detective or Inquisitor – (Introvert Sensing Thinking Judging)** - They are great problem solvers. This type results from the combination of ISTJ styles.
2. **Nurturer or Therapist – (Introvert Nurturing Feeling Judging)** - They want to help and have talent for feeling what others are feeling. A lot of therapists and police investigators are this type. These type results from a combination of INFJ styles.
3. **Thinker or Skeptic – (Introvert Nurturing Thinking Judging)** - They are quiet and comfortable being alone. They question everything by asking "Why," making them natural-born skeptics. They are a combination of the INTJ styles.
4. **Mr. or Ms. Generous – (Extrovert Nurturing Feeling Judging)** - They are focused individuals who look to the future. They are a combination of the

ENFJ styles.

5. **Builder or Architect – (Introvert Sensing Thinking Perceiving)** - They like to stay behind the scenes and direct the foundation. They can be spontaneous, but that spontaneity is never reckless, it's more of a planned diversion. They are a combination of ISTP styles.

6. **Keeper or Caretaker – (Extrovert Sensing Feeling Judging)** - They are the epitome of the extrovert, with a sense of responsibility to family and friends. Even though they are the life of the party, they know where their bread is buttered. They are a combination of the ESFJ styles of learning and perception.

7. **Watcher or Observer – (Introvert Nurturing Feeling Perceiving)** - They are thinkers that do not like attention or to speak about themselves. They are a combination of the INFP styles.

8. **Ringmaster or Actor – (Extrovert Sensing Feeling Perceiving)** - They are performers and natural-born entertainers. As you may have guessed, a lot of actors, comics, and musicians are this type. They are a combination of the ESFP styles.

9. **Mr. or Ms. Success – (Extrovert Nurturing Feeling Perceiving) -** They do it their way all the time and prefer to separate themselves from the crowd. They prefer highly individualistic people and tend to be entrepreneurial. They are a combination of the ENFP styles.

10. **Worker or Busy Bee – (Extrovert Sensing Thinking Perceiving)** - They aren't usually leaders or the take-charge type but prefer to make action happen by taking the direction of others. They are a combination of the ESTP styles.

11. **The CEO or Boss – (Extrovert Sensing Thinking Judging)** - They have a drive to succeed and will take charge to ensure that happens. They are a combination of the ESTJ styles.

12. **General or Admiral – (Extrovert Nurturing Thinking Judging)** - They are natural-born leaders and usually follow a strict code of conduct and ethics. They are a combination of ENTJ styles.

13. **Scholar or Professor – (Introvert Nurturing Thinking Perceiving)** - They are theorists and love to teach and learn. Many scientists and teachers come from

this type. They are a combination of the INTP styles.

14. **Giver or Patron – (Introvert Sensing Feeling Judging)** - They love to give and are never hesitant to lend a helping hand. Their stuff is your stuff, within reason. They are a combination of the ISFJ styles.

15. **Explorer or Designer – (Extrovert Nurturing Thinking Perceiving)** - This type is the rarest in the world, which is completely understandable. They really try to avoid large-scale gatherings and prefer smaller groups. They love to learn and are a combination of the ENTP styles.

16. **Author or Inventor – (Introvert Sensing Feeling Perceiving)** - They are introverts that have a lot of extroverted tendencies. The love to create, design, and break new ground, and are a combination of the ISFP styles.

Are you curious as to what type you are? Then take the original Myers Briggs Assessment and come on back.

As you can see the types of personalities are many and can be daunting, so many behavioral scientists have opted for the more concise method of just grouping their traits or behaviors together to define someone, rather than observing learning styles. This will be the subject of the following section. Still, having a greater understanding of how a person takes in information will equip you to fully understand how a friend or partner thinks. That can be a huge advantage and will cut down on the guesswork often associated with relationships and allow you to put out the best type of energy.

Personality Traits

The major personality traits or behavior patterns that we are about to look at are defined by many psychologists as the Five Factor Model. Many people possess a mix of each of these, but one always tends to dominate. Where the personality types (from the previous section) key us in on how a person should behave, this takes into consideration how they **do** behave as its measure. These arise from a need to simplify the personality types theory by consolidating the information into smaller groups. They are as follows:

1. **Conscientious** - A person high in this trait will be your Type A personality in that they are efficient, a planner, driven, organized, and ambitious. They like to do things by themselves and have a hard time delegating. If you are someone that likes to fly by the seat of their pants, then you may see this person as tedious and hard to please.

2. **Extrovert** - This type of person is high energy, extremely outgoing, and loves to be the center of attention. The quintessential social butterfly, so if you are introverted or reserved, then they may overwhelm you.

3. **Agreeable** - People high in this trait are often people pleasers and try very hard to make everyone happy, even to their own detriment. Many people would regard them as a doormat or push over, so if you are mostly comprised of the more dominant types, then this person may appear frail to you. Incidentally, those high in this trait are the most likely to fall victim to a controlling person.

4. **Open to Experience (The Dreamer)** - A person high in this trait will be very creative, imaginative, and prone to seek

new varieties of sensory experiences. They will want to visit new places, try new things, and want a freer life than a planned one.

5. **Neurotic** - Those high in this trait will be emotionally volatile and seek both attention and validation from others. They tend to be anxious and suffer more from negative emotions. If you are a dreamer or extrovert, then you may find this person a downer or too emotionally draining.

Think about both yourself and those closest to you. Are you able put them and yourself into one of the trait groupings or personality types? Which ones? Start to look for patterns between your type and traits and those you love to be around as well as those you don't. If you are noticing those, then you are well on your way to effectively choosing with whom you build relationships, those you avoid, and guessing how your energy may be received or perceived.

Day Eleven: Personality Disorders

Not to be confused with personality types or traits, personality disorders are defined and observed by modern behavioral scientists as chemical, hormonal, or cognitive issues that cause disruption or trouble with mental or emotional functioning. The traits are simply natural tendencies inherent in all people, while disorders can have physical causes and can mostly be treated. People with these types of disorders may have trouble with societal norms and everyday functioning. Though they may be living what society considers a normal life, they can exhibit behaviors or traits that would make them toxic to a great many people. Please bear in mind that they are not "crazy" or to be automatically avoided, but note that the traits exhibited need to be taken into consideration when building your key relationships. The following disorders can be so mild they are never noticed or so severe one can't function at all.

Sadly, most of these disorders are never diagnosed, so the information we have is based on those that do get medical advice and treatment. But through observing those patients, we can learn to see the signs of an undiagnosed disorder. The ten most studied or observed disorders, as defined by the DSM-5

(Medical Diagnosis Book) and listed by Psychology Today are:

1. **Paranoid Personality Disorder** - People suffering from this disorder are extremely paranoid, anxious, and sensitive to others. They look for validation for their fears all around them. It can range from mild to severe.

2. **Schizoid personality disorder** - This disorder causes one to live totally in an internal fantasy world. They seem separated from everything around them and have a hard time accepting reality, so they keep within themselves. The movie the *Secret Life of Walter Mitty* is a severe example.

3. **Schizotypal disorder** - Very much like a Schizoid type, they also suffer from a fantasy delusion, except it leaks into reality and merges with the real world. They see and perceive things that are not there and have a hard time separating reality from fantasy.

4. **Antisocial personality disorder (Sociopath)** - People that suffer from this are completely separated from society's mores and norms. They have little regard for what society considers

right or wrong, they lack a conscious, and follow their own rules. However, they can form positive and loving bonds with select people, while turning off people in the larger sense. Dexter from the Showtime show of the same name is a great (though extreme) example of this disorder.

5. **Borderline personality disorder** - This mainly affects women and can be the result of past abuse, but it causes severe depression and suicidal thoughts. The one bright spot is that due to the symptoms it is often diagnosed and treated. The majority of those suffering from it do respond well to treatment.

6. **Histrionic personality disorder** - This disorder causes feeling of low self-esteem, and those suffering from it have a tendency to be thrill seekers to find satisfaction. They also have a severe reaction to losing or bad news.

7. **Narcissistic personality disorder** - People suffering from this tend to have an exalted sense of importance and can become angry or even violent if that is challenged. They have little sympathy or empathy for others.

8. **Avoidant personality disorder** - This

disorder causes high anxiety and a fear of interacting with others. Those suffering from avoidance will spend a great deal of time worrying about what others think and trying to "read" them. The fear of being ridiculed will render those that suffer the most from this to not want to be with others.

9. **Dependent personality disorder** - Those with this disorder tend to be excessively reliant on others and have a hard time functioning as an independent person.

10. **Obsessive-compulsive disorder (OCD)** - Those suffering from OCD feel they have no control over their situation and may struggle to take control, which results in a lot of frustration and obsessive behavior. They have a warped sense of perfection and tend to live an isolated life in the most extreme cases, like Monk on the USA Network show of the same name.

Remember this is just for your education and to make you aware of both yourself and your surroundings, when it comes to other people. Many people with these disorders lead healthy and happy lives with those that mesh and compliment them. Have you ever known someone with one of these disorders or suspected someone of having one? How did their behavior affect your interaction with them? Did you alter the way you thought or acted toward them to avoid potential conflict? If so, how did that work out?

Case Study: TJ's Story

TJ was diagnosed with OCD at the age of 11 when her mother noticed she would do "odd things" like flip a light switch nine times or rub the wall in a circular fashion before leaving a room. Her 4th grade teacher noticed she would bite down so hard on pencils she would snap them and would turn the pencil sharpener exactly nine times, even if it cut off the lead of the pencil. The school counselor referred her to a local mental health center, where she was diagnosed and began treatment, mostly in the form of counseling. It was discovered that her parents' divorce and the control her mother wielded over her had contributed to a flare up of her condition. TJ learned coping and relaxation techniques and channeled her symptoms in a more productive way. She was a great student and excelled in the Army. Her symptoms eased the more control she attained over her life, and she is now extremely high-functioning and only has mild tendencies during situations that are very stressful.

Day Twelve: A Review Just for You

Today we are going to do a short exercise to review and analyze the information you have collected about yourself and past/current relationships. Remember there are no right or wrong answers here. Feel free to cut and paste this quiz on to a document or just jot your answers down by hand. Keep it handy for later on in the program.

Me: A Snapshot

1. What boundaries are your deal breakers?
2. Which needs rank the highest for you and are they more mental, physical, or emotional?
3. Which dreams of yours take precedence and are they more personal or career oriented?
4. Are your desires more physical

them?

5. What types of relationships are you concentrating on the most?

6. Have you had a toxic experience in that same type of relationship?

7. How did you deal with that toxic relationship (if any)?

8. Considering all of the personality traits, which ones fit you the best and why?

9. Considering all the personality traits, which ones fit the people you are closest to and have the most positive relationships with and why?

A key fact to remember is that personality traits are defining characteristics that are part of all personality types, and they are not to be confused with personality disorders. Disorders are manifestations of recognized inhibitions or normal cognitive/mental/emotional function by way of physical or chemical maladies. They have been followed and observed for years by behavioral scientists, but for most there are no solid treatment plans as in physical disorders. Rather there are accepted courses of treatment from medicine to counselling to coping mechanisms. Sadly, most disorders go undiagnosed, and those that suffer usually develop their own ways of coping. Symptoms range from extremely mild to debilitating.

Those that suffer can be stigmatized in society, which contributes to the lack of treatment. For our purposes, please remember this lesson is merely to help you recognize possible disorders in people you know, so you can make more informed decisions and better relate to them in your life. There is no evidence that those with personality disorders make any less of a contribution to society and relationships as anyone else. Please do not add to the stigma by being fearful of them, it is all about management, as with anything else.

Chapter Key Points:

1. Define the major Personality Traits
2. Traits are recognized as distinct parts of all personalities that define help them
3. Define the major Personality Disorders
4. People with Personality Disorders are not crazy or to be ridiculed

5. Most disorders range from mild (barely noticeable) to severe and debilitating
6. The vast majority of disorders are never treated
7. Chapter and First Half Assessment

Chapter Five: Characteristics of Relationships

Day Thirteen: Toxic Relationships

We have been looking a lot at the characteristics of different people, personalities, and the traits that define their behavior, but we have yet to look at what a toxic relationship and a good relationship looks like from the outside. This will be a key component to choosing partners for any type of relationship going forward. Being able to recognize and define relationships and the people in them will equip you with various skills to discern what you are looking for or not looking for. Setting up a real relationship as a prime example of what to avoid and one that you wish to model is very important.

Let's take a look at a quick guide to what a toxic relationship (of any type) may look like:

1. **One person always seems dissatisfied -** Remember toxic doesn't always mean abusive, though that happens. It can just mean one person's behavior or attitude

is slowly poisoning the other person's attitude or the health of the relationship. One or more persons always seeming miserable or dissatisfied is a sign of toxicity.

2. **They don't talk to each other** - People with a mutually-caring bond care about what the other has to say or what they are feeling. As a result, they talk and communicate, so partners remaining silent and not discussing anything is a sign that one or both of them has become apathetic to the other.

3. **Visible signs of discomfort or passive aggression** - If you see friends or those a part of a romantic couple showing signs of discomfort around each other, like flinching at touch, rolling of eyes at things they say, or flinging passive aggressive remarks at each other, then that is a sign of issues. The major sign in this category is one of the partners not being consulted for bigger decisions or having their input belittled.

4. **One person is trying harder than the other** - This is consistent behavior that shows one person obviously cares more than the other or others about keeping harmony in the relationship.

5. **Privacy is violated or isolation is actively pursued** - One or more members constantly violate the other's privacy or even check up on the other's whereabouts or activities. Also, any person that is keeping a lover or partner isolated from other people is a huge red flag that something toxic is going on.
6. **Abuse Signs** - Of course this is both glaring and obvious. Any signs of physical or emotional abuse should be taken seriously.

Of course this is a very simple list, but it does consist of valid signs a relationship is in trouble and one or more members may need some help. Think about the relationships around you, whether friends, lovers, or co-workers, and think of any of these signs that occur consistently (every relationship, no matter how good, can have toxic moments, but consistency is the key). Does one or two come to mind? Who? (Don't tell me, just acknowledge it to yourself.) Jot all your ideas about them down and keep them as a model of what not to emulate in the context of a relationship. Did you make note of the attitude or energy that one or more of them put out? How do you think that affected the relationship, if at all?

Day Fourteen: Good Relationships

On the flip side, the signs of a good or great relationship can be just as obvious. These are the types you wish to model and be like in your own. These do not always have to be movie- or novel-like, but just happy and fulfilling. Remember no one is perfect and no relationship is either, but signs of consistent happiness and contentment are obvious and a great thing to see.

1. **They enjoy each other's company** - This is the first and most obvious sign. Happy friends or significant others enjoy hanging out together whether alone or in groups.
2. **They respect each other's privacy and alone time** - Even though they enjoy hanging out together, people that care know everyone needs time alone or with other people in their lives. They respect and allow that time without interference and do not question the other person's intentions.

3. **They speak their truth** - People in a good relationship tell the truth and speak their mind to and in front of each other. This does not lead to conflict or embarrassment on the part of the other. They both care and respect the other's opinions and ideas.

4. **All decisions are mutual** - Everyone inputs, and everyone has a say in major decisions. In the end, if they can't agree, then they compromise and meet in the middle.

5. **They don't linger on the past or arguments** - In short, they don't throw each other's past mistakes in their faces or linger on past disagreements.

6. **They have things in common** - They share similar interests and indulge those interests together as often as possible. I think we often forget that even the most in love couples start as friends, and friends usually have similar interests. Those should be nurtured and not forgotten, no matter how complex life may get.

7. **They show affection** - Not always full-on PDA, but little signs they care are often shown. Whether friends, lover, or family, it's nice to know someone cares,

so don't be shy.

Think of couples in your life that you regard as good or great. These are the ones you want to mimic in your own relationships, so a good way to do that is to mimic what you see them do to each other. A good rule of thumb is to pick two or three traits you observe and attempt to mimic them in your own live (*cough* Law of Attraction *cough*). Take a moment to list their names and what they do that makes them seem like a good example to you.

Case Study: TJ's Story

TJ struggled to come to terms with her own sexuality for many years, and therefore entered into a number of toxic relationships. In her romantic couplings, it had more to do with them being men (who she was not attracted to) and less with the individual in general. As time went on, she became a less talented actress and less able to fake her way through the relationships. Her apparent disinterest in them soon became apparent, and of course that led to a breakdown of the relationships. The same was true of her friendships as she fell back on her religious and very conservative upbringing and sought out like-minded people. Conversely, this was detrimental to her self-esteem and she was confronted with less than welcoming ideas toward gay people. She finally came to terms with being gay, sought out new friends and relationships, and immediately found herself better off than before.

However, things were not all rosy as her first same-sex relationship was with someone who regarded herself better and more attractive than TJ. She regularly put TJ down and suggested everything from makeovers to weight loss. The things they had in common became less important as TJ felt more inadequate and her OCD started resurfacing. Finally, TJ made the painful break, relied on the new friends she'd made, and vowed not to repeat past mistakes by loving herself and making more informed decisions about people.

Day Fifteen: A Self-Assessment

Take the following quiz and use it to paint a portrait of your wants in a relationship.

Me: A Snapshot

1. What do you look for the most in a new friend?
2. What are your favorite hobbies or interests that you would like a friend or significant other to share?
3. Whose relationship do you think is toxic and why?
4. Whose relationship do you think is good or great and why?
5. What of the traits in a good relationship we discussed are the most important to you?
6. Are you willing to treat another person the same way you wish to be treated?
7. Are you willing to make the effort to love and respect yourself as much as you do a friend or significant other?
8. What five things can you do right now to get on a more positive path?
9. Are you ready to get started on learning to love yourself or love yourself more?

If you are, then let's get started on a path to more self-love and learn how to put out the positive energy or attitude that will attract like-minded, positive people.

Chapter Key Points:

1. Identify and Recognize Toxic Relationships
2. Abuse is not always present in Toxic Relationships
3. Identify and Recognize Good Relationships
4. Even the best relationships have toxic moments
5. No relationship or person is perfect, so keep things in perspective
6. Chapter Assessment

Chapter Six: What is Self-Love & Care

In all my years of helping others two of the most neglected areas I see in most people's lives are practicing self-love and self-care. What are these concepts and why are they important?

Many times, people have the habit of not practicing self-love because they have never seen the fundamental role models of their lives do it. How often did you see your mother or father neglect themselves in order to take care of the household? Even if you didn't realize it at the time, that might have become the standard for love in your life. That is why empaths so often show love to others by neglecting themselves. To show love and take care of other is the pinnacle of being a loving/caring person. To neglect yourself is almost a badge of courage and honor. Well, let us start rethinking that in this chapter.

Self-love is defined as having high regard and esteem in oneself, and it doesn't come easy. It is a process that can provide many benefits, such as less stress/depression, higher self-esteem, higher levels of optimism, and more motivation to make beneficial changes in all aspects of one's life. Self-love is often the end product or a welcome side effect of practicing self-care. Self-care is loosely defined as anything a person does to improve the health of their mind and body. It is essential to the survival and well-being of any person.

Even though this course and book is centered on building better relationships, we cannot ignore some basics of self-care that must be kept in mind as we continue this journey. A person who cares for themselves the best they can is someone that will care for loved ones in the same way. Here are the basics of showing yourself love and care:

1. **Learning your self-worth** - Self-worth is a hard a thing to pinpoint, but your worth is as valuable as anyone else in your life, if not more so. You cannot begin to be a caretaker of others before you know your own value.
2. **Stress management** - Learning to reduce stress is a major tool in self-care. Choosing non-destructive outlets to de-stress is key, as well as techniques to help reduce stress like meditation and deep breathing.
3. **Improving physical health** - Eating a balanced diet, exercising, getting

adequate sleep, and drinking the right amount of water daily are vital to keeping a healthy body and, in turn, a healthy mind and spirit.

4. **Changing your environment** - If something in your space is bringing you down or just seems lacking, then make some changes. Add color, photos, stuffed animals, or anything that would brighten your day. The Law of Attraction applies here as well, as what you take in, you will put out.

5. **Take a moment** - Reassess your situation. Have there been major changes to your situation that you have not yet digested? It is always good to slow down and do some thinking, as your plan may need some adjusting.

Now that you know the basics about what makes people behave the way they do, the fundamentals of relationship types, and an idea of the type of relationship you want, we can delve deeper by getting into self-care, self-love, and making time for love for the purpose of moving into stronger and more positive relationships.

Day Sixteen: Shaking off the Past

No matter who you are or your status in life, you have a past that is filled with both good and bad, success and failures. The common fact that holds most people back is that they cannot move on or let go of the past. This is true for both success and failures. Believe it or not, even holding on to past victories or successes can create strife in your current life or perception, because you tend to base your current situation on the past. It may prevent you from making necessary changes to your current project, based on the fact that you had a success last year. People tend to blot out the niche details, like a different client, requirement, or purpose.

The same is true of relationships. Have you ever gotten over-confident about a possible new friend or significant other based on a past relationship and not considered the actual person or situation? Don't worry, we all have - it's just human nature. The same is true over past failures or toxic relationships, as we tend to assume that because of a bad experience or toxic partner, that no one else would want to associate with us, so why bother trying. We overlook our current circumstances and the individual person based on past perceptions.

To help avoid this in the future, here are a few steps you can use to make sure you don't let the past cloud the present or future:

1. **Breathe, smile, and let go of the past situation** - Let the song from Disney's *Frozen* be your guide and "Let it Go." I know it's easier sung or said than done, but it can be a reality. It's key to remember that no matter what, the past is over and should be learned from, not feared. Nothing you do in this moment will change the past situation but letting go of the negative feelings will enable you to see your present clearly.
2. **Accept your responsibility** - Learn from the mistakes you made in the past and accept it as your responsibility, do not let it cloud your present judgement. Take what you learned and use it to better your present.
3. **Forgive yourself** - Something bad happened and that is horrible, but now you must forgive yourself for being in the situation. You are not a victim forever, but a strong person capable of both forgiving yourself and allowing

yourself to be happy.

4. **Forgive those that hurt you** - Part of moving on is forgiving others that have hurt you and not allowing their wrongs to hurt your present and future. When you hold on to bad feeling about yourself or others, it prevents good ones from forming.

5. **Live in the present and for the future** - The past is, well, in the past, and it is over. Learning to concentrate on what is happening now is a vital skill. It enables the joy of the moment to come in and paints a hopeful picture of the future.

I know this may be a difficult exercise, but please write down one or two painful instances from your past. Are you ready to let it go and move on? If the answer is "yes," then let's start by admitting that it happened and naming anyone else that may have been involved. Now, be honest with yourself about your current feelings of the situation or relationship. What things remain undone in your opinion? Is it possible to get those things taken care of (like closure or an apology)?

If so, what are the logical steps to achieve it and are you prepared to take those steps? If nothing is left undone or it can't be achieved, what steps can you take to move on? Ask yourself these questions:

1. Is this a cloud over my current life?
2. Would tying up the loose ends improve my current life?
3. Am I capable of leaving this in the past and living in the present?
4. Can I love and respect myself enough to forgive myself and others?
5. Am I prepared to do this?

Did this open up a huge Pandora's box for you or did it release enough baggage that you can see the path forward? It may be painful, but we must let go of the past to embrace the future. Take a piece of paper and write down the most traumatic toxic relationships on it. Now fold it, rip it up, and scatter the pieces in a stiff breeze (or if it makes you feel better, then shove it down the garbage disposal), whatever it takes let it go. Start to adjust your thinking of these situations from viewing them as a failure to an opportunity to change your thinking and actions in regard to forming new bonds.

Day Seventeen: Putting Your Needs First

Are you an empath? Don't worry, it's not a bad thing or something for which to be ashamed. It is simply someone that feels for others, rather than feeling for themselves. Empaths tend to put the needs of everyone else in front of their own, often to their detriment. They are consummate caregivers and derive satisfaction from helping others. There is nothing wrong with having this kind of nature in general. However, the issue arises when you tend to give so much to others that you have nothing left for yourself and your own health or mental well-being suffers. Remember the example of the parents neglecting themselves for the good of others that you may have modeled yourself after? While that may seem selfless on the surface, in reality, it is a very dangerous arrangement that can lead to a total meltdown of the giving empath. This will result in a situation of neglecting themselves by excessively focusing on others and an overall deterioration of their own mental/physical health. Other than tradition or feeling, there are several reasons why an empath may engage in this type of behavior.

1. **They believe they will lose the favor of people** - That may happen, or it may not, but one thing is clear: any person

who only likes you because of what you do for them is not a person you need in your life. They are toxic by definition and getting them out of your life will free up necessary time for yourself.

2. **It gives them a sense of self-worth** - Helping others makes them feel good about themselves and almost gives them a purpose for living. Though there is nothing wrong with taking pride in caring for others, remember to take pride in caring for yourself.

3. **They feel other people are their responsibility** - This is very true in the case of minor children or perhaps a disabled adult you care for, but an adult is not responsible for another adult, in most cases. People should be able to care for themselves and not be dependent on another to an extreme degree. This aspect of being an empath can walk the line between a caring nature and co-dependence.

Be honest, are any of these you or anyone you know? If so, here are some techniques you can use to help remember to put you first:

1. **Be mindful of your needs or wants** - Listen to your needs and wants and be

mindful of what your mind and body is telling you. Make sure meeting those is a priority for you.

2. **Be selfish on occasion** - It's okay to feed yourself before feeding others or put your own mask on before helping another. If you allow yourself to take care of yourself, then you'll have more to give others when warranted.

3. **Make time for yourself** - Get your personal time in and leave time for your hobbies and interests. A satisfied mind is a satisfied person, and it will make you a better person overall.

4. **Learn to say "no"** - It's okay, you can't be everything to everyone, so please don't try. Take care of yourself and you'll be better for those who really love and need you.

5. **Shift your life view** - Instead of viewing your worth through the needs/eyes of others, view your life through your own eyes. Make yourself what you want you to be, and do not measure your worth by how others treat you.

If you practice these techniques you will reap some important mental and physical benefits, like these:

1. **You'll be more productive** - More time for you means more time for your projects.
2. **You'll be more happy** - Simply put, if your needs are met, then you'll have a better outlook.
3. **More energy and less stress** - Self-care can lesson many of the doubts you may have about your own abilities and energize you for meeting those new expectations.
4. **More respect from others** - People who care for themselves carry themselves in a more positive way. This will earn respect from other positive people.
5. **Better relationships and less resentment** - Isn't this why you are taking the course? Attracting other positive people will result in better relationships, and you will find your relationships improve because you feel less taken advantage of when you address your own needs, thus eliminating resentment.

Are you ready to start practicing some of these? If so, then get started today! Take some time for yourself and do not overload yourself with tasks for others. Jot down some ways you could do this starting today. It is never too late to start a self-care or self-improvement plan with very simple steps that may open up a world of new emotions and opportunities for you.

1. **Start taking walks** - Nothing clears my head like an early walk on a cool morning. Whether I am listening to my favorite tunes or just listening to the sounds of the neighborhood waking up, it sets a positive tone for my day.

2. **Take a Yoga or Stretching class** - The basic Yoga class I take once a week enables me to meet new people (I have met several new friends) and give my body a beneficial stretch from the work week. I always leave feeling energized!

3. **Learn an Art or Craft** - Discovering creativity within yourself is a huge mind stimulator, and it gives you another outlet to express yourself.

4. **Play with your pet** - Enough said! Puppies and kittens are cute, and studies show they have health benefits like lowering blood pressure and adding to one's overall life-span. You can rest assured that your pet is not

judging you and loves you unconditionally, so spend time with them.

5. **Take short breathing breaks** - Take a break a few times a day just to take some deep breaths. You'll be shocked by how much it centers you.

6. **Make time for the essentials** - Have you ever forgotten to brush your teeth or ran out without showering because you were taking care of everyone else? Of course you have. You love others and want to care for them, but don't neglect yourself. If you make yourself unhealthy by neglect or your self-esteem suffers due to it, then that will have a detrimental effect on everyone.

You are great at taking care of others, so now take care of you!

Day Eighteen: Take Time for Fun

All work and no play makes anyone dull, ad this is true even if your career goals (from earlier in the book) are your priorities. Anyone that works all the time and pursues nothing but work-related activities will develop a resentful and pessimistic attitude. There is a reason that the term "burnout" exists, and that is because you can work too much. It is easy to confuse just being a hard worker with "workaholism," but they are not the same. Working hard is simply what it says, giving maximum effort at your job for maximum return. You may be thinking, "Why is working hard a bad thing," and I am not saying that it is. In fact, having an engaging and stimulating job can be a great thing and add to one's sense of worth.

Recent studies show that Americans and the Japanese have the poorest work/life balance in the modern world. They leave a staggering 52 billion hours in unused vacation time on the books on a yearly basis and have an average work week of 55 hours. This is in stark contrast to the citizens of many Western European countries, like France, with an average work week of 35 hours. I realize that some of this is economically driven as many people must work overtime or multiple jobs to make ends meet, and if that is your position, then it may be unavoidable, and you do not need to beat yourself up about. However, please ensure you take care of yourself and pamper yourself on occasion.

It's when work becomes the driving force for everything you do and takes precedence over everything else in life that it becomes a problem. Just like becoming dependent on a person for your self-esteem is toxic, so is becoming dependent on a job, project, or career. Here are some signs and symptoms of being a workaholic:

1. You actively attempt to free up more time to work.
2. You spend much more time working than in any other activity by design.
3. You work in order to reduce or deal with emotional or family issues.

Sounds very much like dependence on drugs or alcohol, doesn't it? Is this you? If it is, then we need to give you some techniques to avoid slipping into the state of extreme workaholism.

1. **Get a hobby** - Or rekindle your passion for a past one. The self-satisfaction that comes from engaging one's interests is immeasurable and leads to more happiness and contentment overall. It

will also stimulate your mind and help your endorphins start to bubble, which makes you happy.

2. **Designate a time to shut it down** - It doesn't have to be 5 pm on the dot, but if you find yourself at the office at 7 pm each night, then maybe you need to plan a time to eject yourself. Make sure you stick to it. Have a friend hold you accountable by calling or texting you. Leave when that happens, do not get frustrated or ugly with them.

3. **Find other outlets to deal with stress** - Instead of disappearing into the world of work to deal with things, find another outlet. Talk to a friend, take a bath, workout, or watch a movie. There are many other things besides work that can take your mind off of unpleasant things.

4. **Meditate or practice other relaxation techniques** - Moving and relaxing the body are great ways to release stress and center yourself. Also, these kinds of things will have positive physical effects on you, such as improving circulation, muscle flexibility, and releasing tension.

5. **Workout** - Exercise has tremendous physical benefits, including the release

of endorphins that improve mood. Also, it can improve the shape of you and help you lose those pesky pounds. That always gives self-esteem a little boost as well as improve your health and endurance.

6. **Hang out with family and friends** - Remember them? They want to see you and have a good time. Studies have shown that those with a close circle of family and friends have a more satisfying life and live longer.

Which of these techniques could you start today, this week, or this month? Can you find a way to make time for yourself and have fun? I hope so because it will bring out the positivity that lies underneath and other positive people will notice.

Case Study: TJ's Story

After the end of her first same-sex relationship, TJ threw herself into her work, and all her activities (social and otherwise) revolved around it. Her only social activities or non-work outlets were going out with work friends. Soon, her routine was work, drink, and sleep. And as a result, she was drinking daily. She didn't even realize the extent until she was arrested for a DUI. That served as a wake-up call and she changed to another, less stressful career, while starting to pursue things like working out and hobbies. One of those hobbies was doing standup comedy (which she did in college). She found a new happiness and started to pursue it as often as possible. She also met new people and made new friends with similar interests, among them was the woman to whom she would eventually be happily married. Don't worry, we will finish the story later.

Chapter Key Points:

1. Learning to not dwell on the past and how to do it
2. Defining Self-Care and Loving yourself
3. Learning techniques to practice self-care
4. Overcoming barriers to having fun and workaholism

Chapter Seven: Self-Analysis & Affirmations

Who are you? That's a question that has been asked by therapists, psychologists, and in psychology classes for over 100 years. It is a multifaceted question that asks a person to dive deep into their own self and make a determination of identity. It is vital to know who you are before you can know someone else. Now that you've learned how to care for and respect yourself, it's time to put the rubber to the road and figure out what else makes you tick. It's these things that will enable you to know yourself well enough to attract the right kinds of people for you.

The purpose of the self-analysis process is to highlight core strengths (dominant traits), understand weaknesses (smaller or less dominant traits), and develop those traits that are not natural or dominate in you. In order to do this, you must be willing to recognize areas that need improvement or development. Those traits that are not dominate can be learned and improved upon (as shown in Day Nineteen).

Please remember that, for standard analysis purposes, traits are grouped as strengths or weaknesses, but this is not a slight to you if

114

you have more that rank as weaknesses than strengths. It is merely a tool to help you better understand what traits you possess and what complementary traits your potential relationships should have.

Day Nineteen: Basic Self-Analysis

There are many complicated formulas and tests for self-analysis that you can find online easily with a simple search, but here we are going to keep it simple. Basically, a self-analysis is made up of what you think of yourself and, in some cases, what other think of you. We will only focus on the self part for our purposes. Basically, self-analysis breaks your personality down into strengths and weaknesses based on a list of traits, an example of which I am placing below from edrawsoft.com.

Adaptable	Aloof	Aggressive	Amiable	Ambitious
Anxious	Arrogant	Assertive	Assured	Careful
Cheerful	Co-ordinated	Co-operative	Competitive	Confident
Considerate	Creative	Daring	Decisive	Dependable
Determined	Easy-going	Emotional	Encouraging	Enterprising
Extrovert	Fickle	Forceful	Forthright	Friendly
Generous	Gregarious	Hard Worker	Helpful	Honest
Humorous	Ill-tempered	Independent	Innovative	Introverted
Judicious	Kind	Lazy	Mild-manner	Objective
Obstinate	Open-mind	Orderly	Original	Patient
Passionate	Persistent	Prudent	Reliable	Reticent
Self-conscious	Self-reliant	Shy	Sincere	Systematic
Tactful	Tenacious	Trustworthy	Optimistic	Pessimistic

The main objective of an analysis is to rank each of the traits listed above on a scale of one to ten. Those appearing from one to five are considered minor traits, or weaknesses, while those rating six to ten are major traits, or strengths. Take a few minutes and rank yourself now. There's no hurry and there are no wrong answers, this is just an exercise to help you more clearly see what traits you have (like in Day Ten) rather than just guessing. Go ahead and start ranking the traits by placing a value of one to ten next to them.

Are you surprised by the results or are they pretty much on par with what you thought? Now, separate the Stronger Traits from the

Weaker Traits, so we can form a plan for changing those in the weaker list into strengths. This is also true for strengths ranking a bit lower (6 or 7) that you wish to make stronger or those that you wish you weren't that strong in to be moved lower. Also, bear in mind that some things in the weaker list should stay there (for example, pessimistic), so this is only for those that you would like to move to the stronger column. This is called taking an inventory, and it's just like the type you would create at work for products or supplies to see what needs to be restocked. It is no different for you, it is just the restocking process is a little more personal. Here are the remaining steps in the process, with examples:

Inventory   Strengths   and Limitations/Weaknesses

1. **Set Goals** - For which items or traits you wish to work on first.
2. **Obtain a Coach or a Mentor** - If you need help, then ask for it. Turn to a trusted friend or someone at work you look up too that has the strength you are seeking to improve.
3. **Reward Yourself** - Once you accomplish a step on the way to your

goal, reward yourself and give yourself the praise you deserve.

Sample Self-Assessment

Adaptable-8	Aloof-6	Aggressive-4	Amiable-6	Ambitious-10
Anxious-9	Arrogant-6	Assertive-8	Assured-7	Careful-9
Cheerful-9	Coordinated-6		Competitive-4	Confident-8
Considerate-6	Creative-8	Daring-7	Decisive-6	Dependable-9
Determined-9		Emotional-9	Encouraging-9	Enterprising-9
Extrovert-6	Fickle-4	Forceful-3	Forthright-9	Friendly-8
Generous-9	Gregarious-4	Hard Worker-9	Helpful-8	Honest-9
Humorous-9			Innovative-8	Introverted-7
Judicious-4	Kind-8	Lazy-3		Objective-8
Obstinate-1	Open-mind-8	Orderly-8	Original-9	Patient-3
Passionate-9	Persistent-9	Prudent-8	Reliable-9	Reticent-5
Self-conscious-3	Self-reliant-9	Shy-9	Sincere-7	Systematic-6
Tactful-6	Tenacious-7		Optimistic-7	Pessimistic-4

Looking at the above example, pick out the ones you wish to change by moving into a stronger position on the list, like below:

Patient-3

Tactful-6

Aloof-6

Now it is time to start your improvement plan, which is a very simple process:

1. Brainstorm ideas for how to proceed.
2. Prioritize your goals (by picking the things you wish to change first).
3. Concentrate on a single goal at a time (do not try to do too much at once).
4. Research how to get started on your goal.
5. Get started on the process.
6. Take stock of how you are progressing and reward yourself for progress made.

This needn't be a stressful situation, it's more of an exercise to improve on points you desire to change. Change isn't easy, so go easy on yourself and give yourself adequate time to adapt and make the changes permanent. Remember it takes about 100 days for something to become a habit, so give yourself time. You are well on your way to understanding what makes you tick.

Day Twenty: Affirm Yourself

Change can be difficult, and how you adapt to change is key. Most of us have only one major enemy and that is ourselves. Have you ever heard an idea that is based on some sort of significant change to your routine, career path, or location, and then immediately began throwing up obstacles to it? Reasoning as to why it is just not feasible for you or that it is not a solid idea, even if it is a great thing for you and your family. That's where self-affirmation comes in which is simply how individuals adapt to information or experiences that are threatening to their self-concept.

How positive your self-affirmation is can be a great indicator of how much of your self-identity is wrapped up in your own internal ideas versus how much is wrapped up in external factors. It is when the emphasis is too firmly concentrated on outside factors that there is danger to you. When you depend on outside circumstances or other people for your own self-identity or worth, it places you in a position to be easily taken advantage of and to choose people that will be toxic for you without resistance. So, it is vital that you affirm yourself internally and know your own worth or value, no matter what is going on around you.

In other words, you are more than your job, friends, home, lovers, and location. There are many things that occur in life that no one can control. Layoffs, breakups, moves, children's behavior, and grades can only be controlled to a certain degree or extent. Once you accept that, it will be much easier to separate your own self-worth from the external factors that no one has full control over. You are more than the sum of your parts or accomplishments, much more.

So, how do you improve your self-affirmation if it is weaker than it should be? Much like we discussed in Day Nineteen, it has a lot to do with habits and being self-aware of who you are. Things become a habit after 100 days of doing it or hearing it, and that's where our exercise comes in. We will learn to construct and use our own personalized daily affirmations, which will help to change our way of thinking.

Classical affirmations, as used by motivational speakers, are short, powerful, simple statements designed to encourage a life and fill it with positivity. A daily morning affirmation can be as simple as "I am good enough" or "I will conquer this day." They are more than just self-help statements, as they can have a significant impact on our overall quality of life. Using them regularly allows you to become more in tune with the way you think about yourself, in general. So, it is not the affirmation itself that creates positivity, but the awareness of your own thought patterns that allows you to make continuous changes to improve your state of mind. This happens in a couple of different ways:

1. They make you aware of any self-statements, whether positive or negative. It then allows you to affirm the positive and adjust the negative by simply changing it from a declarative "I am" statement to an interrogative "Am I" or "Is this" question. This aids in giving you a plan for changing the negative statements to questions, then into positive statements.
2. It gives you time to examine possible answers to these questions and come up with additional questions that will allow you better insight.

Examples would be changing "I am not worthy of love" to "Am I worthy of Love" or "Why do I think I am not worthy of love." You can see how this would cause some deep questioning and give you more items to add to your self-assessment/improvement plan. Basically, we are just trying to reframe how you think about yourself in a pragmatic way. You can use affirmations in a variety of situations. These might include times when you want to raise your confidence, control negative feelings, improve your self-esteem, finish a project, or overcome a bad habit. Let's begin by jotting down the first ten thoughts about yourself that come to mind. Write them down exactly as they come, then look at them to determine whether they are positive or negative. How could you turn the negatives into positives or reframe them so you can make a plan to improve your opinion in that matter?

Here is an example:

1. I am unattractive. -> Why do I think I am unattractive?
2. I am not capable of completing this work project. -> What steps can I take to complete this project?
3. I feel unintelligent next to some of my co-workers. -> What specifically do these co-workers do that makes me feel unintelligent and how can I mimic that?

Try to reform and rework your thoughts every day. It will lead to better thoughts and a better outlook for your future. Okay, we all love the motivational types of affirmations, and let's face it they are very nice to read, and they do adjust your thinking a bit. So, here is a list of some basic affirmations you can use to give yourself a bit of a boost:

- I accept myself.
- I believe in myself.
- I will learn to eat well, exercise regularly, and get plenty of rest going forward.
- I learn from my mistakes and do not accept blame for the errors of others.
- I can accomplish anything I set my mind to.
- I forgive myself.
- I will never give up.
- I accept what I cannot change and change what I can.
- I make the best of any situation I find myself in.
- I laugh at myself.
- I enjoy life to the fullest.
- I have control over my choices.

Try reciting these and developing some of your own!

Case Study: TJ's Story

After starting to perform stand-up comedy, TJ had some initial success but started to doubt herself a bit when she wasn't getting booked as often as she thought she should. So, as was her pattern, she got down on herself. Daily, she would bombard herself with thoughts like "I am not good enough" and "No one will like me." She began to get depressed and not try as hard to book shows or auditions. In addition, her day job and other projects began to suffer from her negative outlook. Finally, she decided to take it day by day and try to have a positive attitude as much as possible. Instead of dwelling on what she thought were the negative aspects of herself, she would figure out how to improve them, and gradually the negative statements became questions then positive statements. These statements gradually turned into positive behavior and results for her.

Chapter Key Points:

1. Define Self-Analysis

2. Conduct a basic Self-Analysis and Inventory
3. Categorize and identify your Strengths and Weaknesses
4. Take the sample Self-Assessment
5. Define Self-Affirmation and how it can be used for Self-Approval
6. Construct your own daily Affirmations

Chapter Eight: Learn to Love Again

We are now starting the most difficult part for any empath or introvert, and that is learning to love others again or allowing others to love you. So often, empaths are quick to downplay the role they play in the lives of others by not accepting the fruits of another person's love. They are quite content to love and care for others, while not acknowledging or outwardly receiving their loved ones' feelings for them. Not allowing others to return your love can create an unbalanced relationship and cause feelings of inadequacy in the other person, due to the empath's compulsion to shoulder all the emotional baggage.

We have all had at least one person in our lives that has loved us unconditionally, and if you think hard enough, you can feel that warmth. Can you see them, see their smile, and perhaps hear their voice? Dwell on that and remember how they made you feel. Now don't you want to feel that again? If you do, then you must let others love and care for you, as much as you care for them. In this chapter, we will explore how to allow that and to open yourself up for the love and affection you deserve. A good starting point for this section is to pretend to be that person you were just thinking about and focus the love they have or had for you outward, as if it is your own.

Day Twenty-One: Giving and Receiving Love

Let others return the favor

You are probably thinking "I don't need lessons on loving others, I have been doing it all my life." It may be true that you have cared for others, but have you really loved them? I mean in a true, honest, and fair way without judgement or resentment toward others for daring to tread into your territory. What exactly does that mean? Is true love unfair and does it cause resentment? Well, unrequited love is quite unfair to the person on the outside, isn't it? What about resentment? Well think about all the times you or someone you know has shown love and service to others, while not allowing them or wanting them to return the favor. Not being allowed to return love and affection can certainly build resentment in both parties. On the part of the person that is not allowed to show love for not being able to, and on the part of the one showing all the love, when they begin to think they are not cared for.

So how do you avoid these situations? Make sure you know your worth (think about all the great things we have learned in the past nineteen days) and do not lose yourself in another person or become codependent with someone else. As we have discovered in the past few chapters, anytime you start to define yourself or see your self-worth only through others' treatment of you that it is a recipe for toxicity. Any relationship, whether family, casual, platonic, or romantic, should be symbiotic or mutually beneficial to all members.

Don't Smother Others

No one should be unfairly burdened with the majority of the love in any relationship nor should anyone person be smothered by affection. Yes, that is possible, and it can lead to the breakdown of a relationship.

What is smothering someone? What does that

look like? Simply put, to smother someone with love is to dote or protect them to the point that they cannot care for themselves or independently move within the relationship. Has that ever happened to you or do you tend to do it to others? To be sure here are some signs of "smothering a person:"

1. One partner, family member, or friend is withdrawing from the other person.
2. Others tell one of them that they may be smothering someone.
3. The smothering person doesn't feel comfortable or like being separated from the other person or doing things on their own
4. The smothering person never feels like they can get close enough or do enough for the other friend, family, or partner.
5. One or more of them say they feel suffocated in the relationship.

That doesn't sound very nice or warm, does it? What are some of the things that can be done to prevent smothering in your family, friendships, or other relationships. Here is a brief list that I have gleaned from my years of helping and coaching others:

1. Take time for yourself.

2. Give your partner, family member, or partner a sufficient amount of time, space, and room to breathe.
3. Balance your needs for caring and being with them with their need for alone time and space.
4. Enjoy your own interests.
5. Stay in touch with yourself.
6. Remember you are worth it, and you shouldn't have to overdo affection to get love in return.
7. Take time away from your partner or family and encourage them to do the same.
8. Cultivate and mix with your own friendships and friends.
9. Know who you are as a person (all the things you have learned in the previous days are key here).
10. Develop your own personal, social, and professional identity.

It is so important for everyone to have a strong sense of independence and a life/identity of their own. When two independent people come together in relationship, they bring their own unique experiences and preferences which, when they mingle symbiotically, can create a strong bond. It's when the balance becomes warped or slanted toward one or the other that someone will feel undervalued, overly absorbed, or obsessed. This will feed the toxicity, which will begin to simmer. You have heard the old adage "you can lead a horse to water, but you can't make him drink," well that is very true in relationships. You can only do what you can do and nothing more, so being overly focused on showering love and affection on a person or group of people is a useless exercise. No matter what you do or how much you do it if the feeling isn't mutual or the other person feels smothered, then it will not work out. If you are putting out love and love is not coming back (and never has), then that is a sign that the relationship is not right.

How Much Affection is Right or What Language do you Speak?

You are probably wondering exactly how much affection is the right amount? Well, I cannot answer that with an equation like $XY + (3x - 2y) = LOVE$, as love and feelings are not a science. It's more of a craft that is honed over years of experience, with a great deal of it being ingrained from an early age. The great thing is that, unlike personality, the level of attention one is inclined to give can be altered and changed as new behaviors and experiences are learned and encountered. Everyone has a different type of personality and traits that go along with them, so that is a good indicator of how they will respond to signs of love/affection and what shape they would need to take.

Though not a strictly scientific study or subject, life coaches and observers of human behavior have pinpointed five love styles or love languages. The term was coined and the distinctions were made in 1995 by Dr. Gary Chapman. In his book *The Five Love Languages,* Dr. Chapman outlines the following distinctions:

1. **Words of Affirmation** - Think of this language as full auditory and based on the love or need to be built up or show affection with words or affirmations. They love to hear words like "I love you" and "You are beautiful," which build them up to ultimate heights. On the flipside, disparaging words or negative phrases can wreak huge damage to the ego and self-esteem of those who speak this language.

2. **Acts of Service** - This is a love language based on actions and providing tangible goods, like providing a cooked meal, doing chores for them, or bringing them coffee. These small acts mean a lot to people who speak this language, but if these things are done with resentment or a sense of obligation, then they can have a damaging effect.

3. **Receiving Gifts** - This differs from Acts of Service in that, instead of providing services or acts of kindness, small gifts are given. Things like occasional flowers, wine, or a night out can mean so much to the person who speaks this language.

4. **Quality Time** - This type of language is based on spending quality, uninterrupted time with your loved one. It is not about the activity, but more about being together and being the total subject of the other's attention.

5. **Physical Touch** - As you may have guessed, this love language is based on touch. Not necessarily sex or physical affection, but just having a physical connection. Something meaningful like touching the arm, holding hands, or a light kiss means so much to those who

speak this language.

How do you know what your love language is and how do you recognize a potential friend or romantic partner? Well, for yourself I suggest the quiz below, but for others it is just observation and reasonable prediction based on their personality type (remember those from Chapter 4). I mean, you can also give them the quiz, but that may come off as a bit weird. Since there is no need to reinvent the wheel, I am placing the link to the original quiz by Dr. Chapman below. Feel free to take it, record your results, and come on back.

Love Language Quiz

Where did you rank on the quiz? What language or love languages do you speak? Are you 100% one or a split of them? How will this affect your current relationships, and will you take new precautions or roads to deciding about future relationships? Now we will take your knowledge and apply it to predicting the love language of others based on your knowledge of their personality type.

Yes, all 16 of the personality types we looked at earlier have a preferred love language or set of languages. So, by the power of your observations and your new deductive skills, you can gauge it from the beginning. Below you will find the personality types (represented by their four-letter learning style representations) and both their primary and secondary love language:

ESFP	Quality Time	Acts of Service
ESTP	Physical Touch	Quality Time
ISTP	Quality Time	Words of Affirmation
ISFP	Quality Time	Words of Affirmation
ISFJ	Physical Touch	Quality Time
ESFJ	Quality Time	Words of Affirmation
ISTJ	Quality Time	Words of Affirmation
ESTJ	Quality Time	Acts of Service
INTJ	Quality Time	Words of Affirmation
ENTJ	Quality Time	Acts of Service

INTP	Quality Time	Physical Touch
ENTP	Quality Time	Words of Affirmation
INFJ	Quality Time	Physical Touch
ENFJ	Quality Time	Words of Affirmation
INFP	Quality Time	Words of Affirmation
ENFP	Words of Affirmation	Quality Time

Looking at the information above, what is the most glaring preference of Love Language?

Above everything, you need to be prepared to spend quality time with people, and as introvert, I know you that scares you. However, that fear can be overcome with a careful and regimented plan. Let's jump into that now in Day Twenty-Two! What, Martha, you said 21 days! 21 days and I'd be ready!? Well, you are ready and fully equipped with all the knowledge you need to discern between the types of people you want to meet and those you want to avoid, but actually doing it is an entirely different plan. So, consider these next few tips a bonus day as we put together a systematic way of getting out into the world of people and become as social as you must to meet your soulmate.

Bonus: Day Twenty-Two

Okay, first we must understand why you are hesitant to get out and meet new people. This is vital as you are seeking new relationships and it is never recommended to specifically seek relationships from only the people you currently know. Not that they are unworthy or bad people, but we as people tend to stay in our safety zone and we miss lots of great opportunities as a result. So, getting out of the safety of people you know is vital to see what is really available for you. Don't worry, if you already know your soulmate, they will make themselves known.

Now what is it that is holding you back from taking a chance? Initially, I am going to say it is because of your personality type or shy traits you possess. Basically, you are an introvert or shy extrovert, and this simply means you either fear or don't enjoy large scale socializing and prefer small groups or solitary activities. This is not to be confused with being shy, which is more of a fear of people or social situations, whereas being introverted just means it's not your first choice of activities. Does that sound like you? If so, then read on, and even if it doesn't like you, then you'll still gain some valuable information.

Introvert vs Extrovert

What are the major contrasts between Introverts and Extroverts? It is not as simple as one is outgoing and one keeps to themselves, as you can see in this chart below.

Extroverts	Introverts
Recharge by being with others	Recharge with alone time
Would rather talk in a group	Would rather talk to one person
Have a lot of less serious friends	Have a few close friends
Love to speak	Love to listen
Okay with change	Freak out with change
Easily distracted	Hard to interrupt
More open with their feelings	Play cards close to the chest
Open up to many	Open up to a few
Decide quickly	Take time to decide

Craves attention	Avoids attention
Willfully volunteer ideas	Respond only when asked

Are you still questioning what you are or where you fall? Then let's take an Introvert Test. Don't worry, this will not forever define you, but will give you a better idea of whether you are an extrovert, introvert, or just shy. There are actually far more extroverts than introverts (by a 3 to 1 margin), so you could very well be an extrovert simply suffering from shyness, but any in case we are going to help you get out there.

Introverts often find that other people try to change them or think they are antisocial or stuck up, but this is hardly the case. Introverts do not hate or fear being in public, they are just more geared for internal reflection and solitude or the company of very close friends. Extroverts tend to be talkative, sociable, friendly, and outgoing. The term social butterfly does not automatically apply, but extroverts tend to thrive in larger groups. They can and do have a need for solitude, but not to the degree of the introvert. On the flip side, they can sometimes be described as attention-seeking, easily distracted, and unable to spend time alone. Some of the major signs of being an introvert instead of an extrovert are:

1. Being with a lot of people tires you out as an introvert, while it recharges you as an extrovert.
2. You need personal time as an introvert but need social interaction as an extrovert.
3. Introverts have a smaller group of intimate friends, while extroverts have a larger group of casual friends.
4. Introverts are often described as hard to get to know or a recluse, while extroverts are often described as loud

and in your face.

5. Introverts tend to be upset or tire easily by large groups, while extroverts thrive off of them.

6. Introverts like to learn by watching, while extroverts tend to learn by doing or interacting.

7. Introverts are drawn to jobs that require little interaction with others, while extroverts crave work in groups or customer interaction.

Can introverts and extroverts be friends or more? Of course! Remember that relationships are a symbiotic arrangement. That simply means that members complement each other and provide each other with needed substance. That means that the outgoing and in-looking contrasts of the two types can complement each other by filling a gap left by the dominant trait. For example, an extrovert can help the introvert learn to socialize, while the introvert can help the extrovert get needed time for reflection. So don't think one has to seek the exact same type, it is all about balance.

Breaking out as an Introvert

What can the introvert or shy extrovert do to get out and about to meet their soulmate? Well, let's take a look at some tips and tricks to do just that:

1. **Pep yourself up or use one of the affirmations we learned earlier** - "I am beautiful, I am smart, and people will love me." Sure, it is a little silly, but it's something I do whenever I walk into an out of the ordinary situation. It gives me the relief and encouragement I need to walk in with a smile on my face.

2. **Use small talk** - Yes, it is rough to do, but it serves the purpose of getting to know people without trampling on anyone's boundaries. Yes, you can avoid it altogether, but then you risk getting in too deep too fast. Small talk can be very useful in the same way that dipping your toe in a pool before jumping in can be. That way, if it doesn't click or chemistry isn't there, then you can walk away with no hard feelings.

3. **Party in moderation** - Introverts tend to get anxious in gatherings or large

groups of people. So, instead of torturing yourself, start small. Make an effort to socialize but start on a very small scale. Start out with lunches or drinks with two to four people and move up from there.

4. **Don't be afraid of random conversations** - The next time you find yourself alone in the work break room, coffee shop, or even the gym, don't be so quick to put on your earphones or earbuds. Stay aware of conversations around you and take opportunities to engage with others around you. Think about it, common ground and interests are important factors in building a strong relationship foundation, so the fact that you are in a common area that interests you both is a good way to strike up an interesting conversation.

5. **Meet new people online** - Introverts can usually communicate better in writing than in person or verbally, at least until they get to know someone. So, join an online page or community page based on something that interests you. This can be sports, food, exercise, politics, and so on, but make sure the topic is not too controversial. Yes, it is

important to meet someone with similar values and beliefs, but getting too deep into opinions on controversies can lead to more toxic than good interactions. The Internet is a safe haven for those that are hesitant to go out and socialize in traditional ways.

6. **Don't pretend to be a social butterfly** - Tell the truth when meeting new people, no matter the circumstances. Remember saying that you love socializing in larger ways, may mean you end up doing just that. Short answer: tell the truth.

7. **Take the spotlight off yourself** - There are two types of people that you will encounter: those who say, "Here I am," and those who think, "There you are." Be a "There you are" person, because that takes the stress off you. Instead of focusing on who is looking at you focus on someone else and you won't feel every prying eye on you.

8. **Understand rejection is nothing personal** - Don't dwell too much on romantic or social rejection as a negative thing. Instead, channel the occurrence as a positive force that removes an incompatible prospect from the fray.

9. **Focus on a hobby and meet people organically through activities** - Be willing to go outside your comfort zone. Learn something new, book a trip to a new place or country, provide your services for a charity you support, or join a club or church. Go to places where people with similar interests and values gather and you are three times as likely to meet someone you mesh with.

10. **Looks are only skin deep** - I know it is cliché, but remember looks fade and personality, values, interests, and a real connection is forever. Try to focus on what will really keep a relationship strong, and don't judge a book by its cover.

Case Study: TJ's Story

TJ was an extrovert but did not know it. Years of living under an overbearing mother, the military, and then a series of toxic relationships had made her forget it. She had retreated into herself and tried not to be noticed. Once she came out of the closet, she did visit bars and clubs to meet new people, but found she had better luck with meeting friends at work or online. She joined a few LGBTQA groups on Facebook and had daily conversations with people like her. Eventually, she took it offline and met some of her online friends in real life, and the result was meeting some life-long friends. Eventually, her love of stand-up took her again, and her friends drug her to an open mic. She had some liquid courage, performed five minutes of stand-up comedy, and was hooked again.

After her set, a young woman came up to her and shyly said she enjoyed TJ's set, to which TJ replied, "Thanks," just as shy. The two chatted for about 25 minutes and exchanged numbers. Over the next few days, they texted back and forth about comedy and animals (a mutual love) and eventually made plans to go to the local zoo. They met, had lunch, more great conversation, and spent a great day together. Eventually, they were inseparable and have now been married for two years. All because one of them stepped out of her comfort zone and meshed with a like-minded person.

Chapter Key Points:

1. Define and understand both Giving and Receiving
2. Grasp the fact you must open yourself up to letting others love you
3. Learn what it is to smother another person and how to avoid it
4. Understanding and defining the Love Languages and how they relate to the major Personality Types
5. Define and describe the terms Introvert, Extrovert, and Shyness and identify yourself as one of them
6. Identify and understand ways an introvert can meet appropriate people.

Chapter Nine: Looking Forward

Summary

We have come to the end of our program, and you have learned a great deal about yourself and skills that will help you recognize those that will respect you and everything you are. In this way, you will use the Law of Attraction to draw your soulmate to you. The Law of Attraction is the belief that "like attracts like," and that by focusing on positivity and having an optimistic outlook, we can bring about similar results. By understanding and following our program, you will be empowered to attract a lifelong partner and great friends. In looking forward, here are some additional tips to make sure you attract the right person:

1. **Be clear about want you want in a partner or friend** - Every toxic relationship has given you new ideas about what you want in your ideal partner or friendships. Sadly, many people focus on the negative instead of

the positive, like focusing on what you do not want instead of what's important. When you focus on what you do not want, then you have a tendency to see those things above anything else. Your power to see only what you want is strong, and you will tend to block out the good parts of a person's character. If a trait or action makes you feel bad, then it is negative. It's that simple. If you find yourself thinking mostly negative thoughts, then use an affirmation to turn it around and focus on the good things about the person (think "Is this person listening to me and respecting my boundaries?").

2. **Focus on it** - Once you have the ideal person's image in your mind, replay it over and over, until one day you will find yourself actually living it. I am not saying to become Walter Mitty or live in your own head, but let that image be in your mind and something you actively search for.

3. **Love Yourself** - The more you focus on what you love about yourself, the more positive thoughts will dominate and will cause you to take positive steps. Others will fall in love with you too,

simply because it feels great to be around people who radiate positivity.

4. **Avoid Jealousy** - Remember to control what you can and don't worry about what you can't. Someone else's connections and associations are prime examples of what you cannot control. Being jealous over others only pushes them farther away and causes you to have less of an opinion of yourself. Instead, focus on you and your ideal partner or friend and move on.

5. **Love takes time** - It is cliché, but true. You just finished this program and your soulmate is not waiting on your porch, but with patience and practicing what you learned, it will happen.

6. **Don't doubt it** - Knowing and believing is a positive energy and lights the way to love and respect, but doubt is a negative energy and creates darkness. When you focus on attracting your soulmate, there is a sense of knowing he/she is on their way.

7. **Live for now** - Don't live just for the future. Yes, focus on what you want, but taking care of yourself and pampering you now is so important. Have a great life today and plan for the

future.

8. **Be the ball** - Or be your future, happily-attached self by not waiting for the relationship to manifest. Think of all the ways in which you can prepare yourself and your life to be in perfect alignment with your soulmate.

9. **Clear out any attitudes** - And beliefs that are holding you back and replace them with your new sense of love and self-worth.

10. **Put yourself first** - Pamper and love yourself, vocalize your boundaries, needs, dreams, and desires.

11. **Be grateful** - You have come a long way by finding the strength and courage to leave a toxic relationship or by deciding that you want more love and positive relationships in your life. Your hard work will make life better for you and everyone around you, and gratitude will help you stay on course.

You are well on your way and will soon find your soulmate. I hope you have enjoyed this program and have learned a lot about yourself and people in general. The human creature is a very complex being with many facets and twists. By understanding the things in this book, you are twenty-one (okay, twenty-two) days closer to finding your soulmate. As you move forward, keep this book handy and refer back to it anytime you need an added boost. The skills you learned in this book are lifelong, as human behavior and personality do not change. In time, you will be able to hone right in on the personality of those you encounter. I wish you much love and luck in your journey.

My final thoughts are that you have the knowledge of people, personalities, and behaviors to make an educated analysis of the types of people you should avoid. This is half the battle, as staying away from potential bad matches will save you a lot of grief. The other half of the battle is that you also have the knowledge to drift towards the right personality types and traits. In addition, you know to gauge a person based on how they mesh with your outlook. Make sure you start with common interests (remember small talk), then progress to discussions about larger things like common values and beliefs. If that is good, then you can analyze how they feel about your boundaries, needs, dreams, and desires. Make sure they respect you and are willing to be supportive (remember actions speak louder than words), all the while you are putting out positivity and happiness. The happy feeling will enter and return from the right person. Psychological Theory, Patterns, and the Law of Attraction will not disappoint and soon you will find your soulmate.

I feel it is fitting to let TJ close out this book with a short work she calls her "Perfect Day." We have gotten snippets from her journey using the Law of Attraction all throughout this book. I hope you see hope and an example to follow for yourself. As a final exercise, write out what would be your perfect day and then strive to have one very soon!

TJ's Perfect Day

This is not a subject that I ever thought I would write about, as I spent the vast majority of my younger life hoping for the future and trying to forget my present. Throughout my life, I lived out my time under the thumb of other people. First a possessive, controlling mother, and then a series of toxic partners. In every one of those situations I lost a piece of myself and forgot how to respect my own boundaries, needs, dreams, and desires.

I joined the military to get away from my homelife and begin the process of being broken down and rebuilt the Army way. Even though I learned a lot and thrived in the Army, I was still living in the future or my hope for a future. Once leaving the military, I moved to a bigger city and finally embraced my well-buried sexuality. It was after the end of a relationship that I finally started rebuilding myself in my own model. I finally started thinking about what I wanted and stepped outside my comfort zone to pursue a lifelong dream. It was through that I met my great friends and beautiful wife, Toshana, and was enabled to experience a perfect day, every day!

A perfect day for me starts with waking up around 6 am, kissing my wife, and taking my dog, Jack, for a long walk. The minute we return, I have a hot cup of coffee waiting for me, courtesy of the timer I set on the coffee pot the night before. This cup of coffee is garnished with Splenda and heavy cream, as I follow the Ketogenic diet.

The coffee is savored while catching up on the news and looking over my schedule for the day. I outline my writing, editing, and virtual assistant projects that must be completed or worked on for the day. Once the coffee cup is empty, I immediately refill it, because... well, you know. I then sit down in front of my laptop, Jack curled next to me in the oversized chair, with either a true crime podcast or show streaming from the TV and begin work by double-checking both my schedule and email.

I start my work day by answering my emails and then plunge into my writing projects that absorb me until noon or so, by which time my wife has risen and begun to prepare for her night shift. We enjoy lunch/breakfast and chat about what is going on. She works nights as a Contracted IT Consultant that does upgrades overnight for clients. We discuss our upcoming road trip for my series of comedy shows through the Midwest.

Yes, I am a stand-up comedian with a successful career, an album, and YouTube following. These trips are always fun, and since both our jobs are very portable, we can make this work. About 1 pm, she goes to her computer in our bedroom to start her night of upgrades and phone calls, while I return to my current writing project. But first, I let Jack out for a romp in the yard and an attempt to catch that pesky squirrel that taunts him from our sunroom window.

At about 6 or 7 pm, I rise from my work and make sure any work due is fully submitted and that I know all my closing/starting points for in-progress work. I then move to the kitchen to begin preparing the evening meal while Jack follows me around the room. Finally, about 8 pm, Toshana and I sit down to enjoy dinner while watching the latest Netflix series that we are binge-watching. We joke and laugh about how some characters are clueless about other characters or how we never saw that twist coming.

She does scold me for occasionally glancing at my work email, but she is only half serious. At about 10 pm we retire to bed, where I watch YouTube (usually on the keto diet or senseless drama channels "spilling the tea" of other channels) videos on my phone while she plays the latest video game sensation with her team on the PlayStation. I drift off to sleep, listening to laser fights and Jack's snoring from the bottom of the bed while looking forward to another perfect day.

Book Summary and Key Points

1. Chapter 1 Key Points

   Types of Abuse - Physical Abuse, Verbal Abuse, Sexual Abuse, Emotional Abuse, Abuse by Omission, Abuse by Commission

   Defining You - Defining, clarifying, and understanding your Boundaries, Needs, Dreams, and Desires

   Refining your Self - Categorizing your Boundaries

2. Chapter 2 Key Points

   Refining your Self - Categorizing your Needs, Dreams, and Desires

3. Chapter 3 Key Points

   Defining Relationships - Categorizing the different types of human relationships

   The Family, Casual Relationships, Friendships, and Romantic Relationships

4. Chapter 4: Defining the Different Personality Types, Traits, and Disorders

   Defining and categorizing the sixteen Personality Types

   Defining and categorizing the five

Understand, form, and define affirmations

8. Chapter 8: Learn to Love Again

Learning to give and receive love within proper limits and how to define those limits

Learning and defining emotional smothering and how to avoid it

Defining and categorizing the Five Love Languages and how they relate to positive relationships

Defining and labeling the concepts of introvert, extrovert, and shyness

Learning to look for love and friendship as an introvert

9. Chapter 9: Looking Forward

Program Summary

TJ's Story, conclusion, and exercise

Useful resources

The Myers Briggs Foundation

The 5 Love Languages

Psychology Today

Mental Health.net

Psychology Today

Boundaries.me

Meet Mindful.com

National Abuse Hotline

Reach Beyond Violence

Conclusion

Hello, I'm Martha McDowell, health enthusiast and happy person.

Thank you for reading this book. I hope it helps you move on from the toxicity of your past, set healthy boundaries, and find your soulmate. The next step is to put all you have learned into practice.

I want to share my experience with as many people as possible so that there could be more happy and healthy people in this world.

Stay healthy!

Kind regards, Martha McDowell

References

American Psychiatric Association (2013). *Diagnostic and Statistical Manual of Mental Disorders* (Fifth ed.). Arlington, VA: American Psychiatric Publishing. pp. 646–49. ISBN 978-0-89042-555-8.

Berrios, G E (1993). "European views on personality disorders: a conceptual history". *Comprehensive Psychiatry*. (1): 14–30. doi:10.1016/0010-440X(93)90031-X. PMID 8425387.

Theodore Millon; Roger D. Davis (1996). *Disorders of Personality: DSM-IV and Beyond*. New York: John Wiley & Sons, Inc. p. 226. ISBN 978-0-471-01186-6.

Bevan, E. & Higgins, D. (2002). Is domestic violence learned? The contribution of five forms of child maltreatment to men's violence and adjustment. *Journal of Family Violence, 17*(3), 223-245.

Bromfield, L. M. (2005). Chronic child maltreatment in an Australian statutory child protection sample (Unpublished doctoral dissertation). Deakin University, Geelong.

Cannon, E. A., Bonomi, A. E., Anderson, M. L., Rivara, F. P., & Thompson, R. S. (2010). Adult health and relationship outcomes among women with abuse experiences during childhood. *Violence and Victims,*

25(3), 291-305.

Chapman, D., Whitfield, C., Felitti, V., Dube, S., Edwards, V., & Anda, R. (2004). Adverse childhood experiences and the risk of depressive disorders in adulthood. *Journal of Affective Disorders, 82*, 217-225.

Chapple, C. (2003). Examining intergenerational violence: violent role modelling or weak parental controls? *Violence & Victims, 18*(2), 143-162.

Chapman, G. D. (1995). The five love languages: How to express heartfelt commitment to your mate. Chicago: Northfield Pub.

Gary Chapman (2009). The Marriage You've Always Wanted. Paperback: 160 pages. Moody Publishers; 1 edition (July 22, 2009). ISBN 978-0802472977.

Gary Chapman, Jennifer Thomas (2013). "When Sorry Isn't Enough". Northfield Press. ISBN 978-0-8024-0704-7

Gary Chapman (2010). *The 5 Love Languages: The Secret to Love That Lasts*. Northfield Press. ISBN 978-0-8024-7315-8.

Gary Chapman, Ross Campbell, M.D. (1997). *The Five Love Languages of Children*. Moody. ISBN 1-881273-65-2.

Gary Chapman, Jennifer Thomas (2006). *The Five Languages of Apology*. Moody. ISBN 1-881273-57-1

Gary Chapman (2009). Love is a Verb: Stories of What Happens When Love Comes Alive Bethany House. ISBN 978-0-7642-0760-0

Gary Chapman, Paul White (2011). *The 5 Languages of*

Appreciation in the Workplace. Northfield Press. ISBN 0-8024-6198-0

Gary Chapman, Paul White & Harold Myra (2014). "Rising Above a Toxic Workplace". Northfield Press. ISBN 978-0-8024-0972-0

Gary Chapman, Paul White & Harold Myra (2014). "Sync or Swim". Northfield Press. ISBN 978-0-8024-1223-2

Clark, C., Caldwell, T., Power, C., & Stansfeld, S. A. (2010). Does the influence of childhood adversity on psychopathology persist across the lifecourse? A 45-year prospective epidemiologic study. *Annals of Epidemiology, 20*(5), 385-394.

Classen, C. C., Gronskaya Palesh, O., Aggarwal, R. (2005). Sexual victimization: A review of the empirical literature. *Trauma, Violence & Abuse, 6*(2), 103-129.

Cohen, M., Deamant, C., Barkan, S., Richardson, J., Young, M., Holman, S. et al. (2000). Domestic violence and childhood sexual abuse in HIV-infected women and women at risk of HIV. *American Journal of Public Health, 90*(4), 560-565.

Ethier, L., Lemelin, J. P., & Lacharite, C. (2004). A longitudinal study of the effects of chronic maltreatment on children's behavioral and emotional problems. *Child Abuse & Neglect, 28*, 1265-1278.

Felitti, V., Anda, R., Nordenberg, D., Williamson, F., Spitz, A., Edwards, V. et al. (1998). Relationship of childhood abuse and household dysfunction in many of the leading causes of death in adults. *American Journal of*

Preventive Medicine, 14(4).

Finkelhor, D., Ormrod, R. K., & Turner, H. A. (2007). Poly-victimization: A neglected component in child victimization. *Child Abuse & Neglect, 31,* 7-26.

Gilbert, R., Spatz Widom, C., Browne, K., Fergusson, D., Webb, E., & Janson, J. (2009). Burden and consequences of child maltreatment in high-income countries. *Lancet, 373,* 68-81.

Graham, J. C., English, D. J., Litrownik, A. J., Thompson, R., Briggs, E. C., & Bangdiwala, S. I. (2010). Maltreatment chronicity defined with reference to development: Extension of the social adaptation outcomes findings to peer relations. *Journal of Family Violence, 25,* 311-324.

Herman, D., Susser, E., Struening, E., & Link, B. (1997). Adverse childhood experiences: Are they risk factors for adult homelessness? *American Journal of Public Health, 87*(2), 249-255.

Higgins, D., & McCabe, M. (2001). Multiple forms of child abuse and neglect: Adult retrospective reports. *Aggression and Violent Behaviour, 6,* 547-578.

Hillis, S., Anda, R., Felitti, V., Nordenberg, D., & Marchbanks, P. (2000). Adverse childhood experiences and sexually transmitted diseases in men and women: A retrospective study. *Pediatrics, 106*(1), 1-6.

Hoermann, Simone; Zupanick, Corinne E. and Dombeck, Mark (January 2011) The History of the Psychiatric Diagnostic System Continued. mentalhelp.net.

Oldham, John M. (2005). "Personality Disorders". *FOCUS*. **3**: 372–82. 10.1176/foc.3.3.372 (inactive 2018-11-04).

Kendell, RE (2002). "The distinction between personality disorder and mental illness". *The British Journal of Psychiatry*. **180** (2): 110–15. 10.1192/bjp.180.2.110.

Jonson-Reid, M., Kohl, P. L., & Drake, B. (2012). Child and adult outcomes of chronic child maltreatment. *Pediatrics, 129*(5), 839-845.

Jung, C. G. (1902–1905). *Psychiatric Studies. The Collected Works of C. G. Jung* Vol. 1. 1953, ed. Michael Fordham, London: Routledge & Kegan Paul, and Princeton, N.J.: Bollingen. This was the first of 18 volumes plus separate bibliography and index. Not including revisions the set was completed in 1967.

Jung, C. G. (1903) "On the Psychology and Pathology of So-Called Occult Phenomena." ("Zur Psychologie und Pathologie sogenannter occulter Phänomene.") His doctoral dissertation.

Jung, C. G. (1904–1907) *Studies in Word Association*. London: Routledge & K. Paul. (contained in *Experimental Researches*, Collected Works Vol. 2)

Jung, C. G. (1907). *The Psychology of Dementia Praecox*. (2nd ed. 1936) New York: Nervous and Mental Disease Publ. Co. (contained in *The Psychogenesis of Mental Disease*, Collected Works Vol. 3. This is the disease now known as schizophrenia)

Jung, C. G. (1907–1958). *The Psychogenesis of Mental Disease*. 1991 ed. London: Routledge. (Collected Works

Vol. 3)

Jung, C. G. (1912). *Psychology of the Unconscious*: a study of the transformations and symbolisms of the libido, a contribution to the history of the evolution of thought. trans. Hinkle, B. M. (1916), London: Kegan Paul Trench Trubner. (revised in 1952 as *Symbols of Transformation*, Collected Works Vol.5 ISBN 0-691-01815-4)

Jung, C. G., & Long, C. E. (1917). *Collected Papers on Analytical Psychology* (2nd ed.). London: Balliere Tindall & Cox. (contained in *Freud and Psychoanalysis*, Collected Works Vol. 4)

Jung, C. G. (1917, 1928). *Two Essays on Analytical Psychology* (1966 revised 2nd ed. Collected Works Vol. 7). London: Routledge.

Jung, C. G., & Baynes, H. G. (1921). *Psychological Types, or, The Psychology of Individuation*. London: Kegan Paul Trench Trubner. (Collected Works Vol.6 ISBN 0-691-01813-8)

Jung, C. G., Baynes, H. G., & Baynes, C. F. (1928). *Contributions to Analytical Psychology*. London: Routledge & Kegan Paul.

Jung, C. G., & Shamdasani, S. (1932). *The Psychology of Kundalini Yoga*: notes of a seminar by C.G. Jung. 1996 ed. Princeton, N.J.: Princeton University Press.

Jung, C. G. (1933). *Modern Man in Search of a Soul*. London: Kegan Paul Trench Trubner, (1955 ed. Harvest Books ISBN 0-15-661206-2)

Jung, C. G. (1934–1954). *The Archetypes and the Collective*

Unconscious. (1981 2nd ed. Collected Works Vol.9 Part 1), Princeton, N.J.: Bollingen. ISBN 0-691-01833-2

Kendall-Tackett, K. (2002). The health effects of childhood abuse: four pathways by which abuse can influence health. *Child Abuse & Neglect, 26*(6-7), 715-729.

Kwong, M., Bartholomew, K., Henderson, A., & Trinke, S. (2003). The intergenerational transmission of relationship violence. *Journal of Family Psychology, 17*(3), 288-301.

Maniglio, R. (2012). Child sexual abuse in the etiology of anxiety disorders: A systematic review of reviews. *Trauma, Violence & Abuse, 14*(2), 96-112.

McQueen, D., Itzin, C., Kennedy, R., Sinason, V., & Maxted, F. (2009). Psychoanalytic psychotherapy after child abuse. The treatment of adults and children who have experienced sexual abuse, violence, and neglect in childhood. London: Karnac Books Ltd.

Miller-Perrin, C., & Perrin, R. (2007). *Child maltreatment: An introduction.* Thousand Oaks: Sage Publications.

Pears, K., & Capaldi, D. (2001). Intergenerational transmission of abuse: A two-generational prospective study of an at-risk sample. *Child Abuse & Neglect, 25,* 1439-1461.

Richmond, J. M., Elliot, A. N., Pierce, T. W., Aspelmeier, J. E., & Alexander, A. A. (2009). Polyvictimization, childhood victimization, and psychological distress in college women. *Child Maltreatment, 14*(2), 127-147.

Rodriguez-Srednicki, O., & Twaite, J. (2006).

Understanding, assessing, and treating adult victims of childhood abuse. Lanham: Rowman & Littlefield Publishers Inc.

Rohde, P., Ichikawa, L., Simon, G., Ludman, E., Linde, J., Jeffrey, R. et al. (2008). Associations of child sexual and physical abuse with obesity and depression in middle-aged women. *Child Abuse & Neglect, 32,* 878-887.

Sachs-Ericsson, N., Cromer, K., Hernandez, A., & Kendall-Tackett, K. (2009). A review of childhood abuse, health, and pain-related problems: The role of psychiatric-disorders and current life stress. *Journal of Trauma and Dissociation, 10*(2), 170-188.

Simpson, T., & Miller, W. (2002). Concomitance between childhood sexual and physical abuse and substance use problems. A review. *Clinical Psychology Review, 22,* 27-77.

Springer, K., Sheridan, J., Kuo, D., & Carnes, M. (2007). Long-term physical and mental health consequences of childhood physical abuse: Results from a large population-based sample of men and women. *Child Abuse & Neglect, 31,* 517-530.

Steel, J., & Herlitz, C. (2005). The association between childhood and adolescent sexual abuse and proxies for sexual risk behavior: A random sample of the general population of Sweden. *Child Abuse & Neglect, 29,* 1141-1153.

Sugaya, L., Hasin, D. S., Olfson, M., Lin, K-H., Grant, B. F., & Blanco, C. (2012). Child physical abuse and adult mental health: A national study. *Journal of Traumatic Stress, 25,* 384-392.

Tam, T., Zlotnick, C., & Robertson, M. (2003). Longitudinal perspective: Adverse childhood events, substance use, and labor force participation among homeless adults. *American Journal of Drug and Alcohol Abuse, 29*(4), 829-846.

Thomas, C., Hypponen, E., & Power, C. (2008). Obesity and type 2 diabetes risk in mid-adult life: The role of childhood adversity. *Pediatrics, 121*, 1240-1249.

Watts-English, T., Fortson, B., Gilber, N., Hooper, S., & De Bellis, M. (2006). The psychobiology of maltreatment in childhood. *Journal of Social Issues, 62*(4), 717-736.

Wegman, H. L., & Stetler, C. (2009). A meta-analytic review of the effects of childhood abuse on medical outcomes in adulthood. *Psychosomatic Medicine, 71*, 805-812.

Whiting, J., Simmons, L. A., Havens, J., Smith, D., & Oka, M. (2009). Intergenerational transmission of violence: The influence of self-appraisals, mental disorders and substance abuse. *Journal of Family Violence, 24*, 639-648.

Widom, C. (1989). Child abuse, neglect, and violent criminal behaviour. *Criminology, 27*(2), 251-271.

Widom, C., Czaja, S., & Dutton, M. (2008). Childhood victimization and lifetime revictimization. *Child Abuse & Neglect, 32*, 785-796.

Widom, C., DuMont, K., & Czaja, S. (2007). A prospective investigation of major depressive disorder and comorbidity in abused and neglected children grown up. *Archives of General Psychiatry, 64*, 49-56.

Widom, C., White, H., Czaja, S., & Marmorstein, N. (2007). Long-term effects of child abuse and neglect on alcohol use and excessive drinking in middle adulthood. *Journal of Studies on Alcohol and Drugs*, 317-325.

Widiger, T. A. (1993). "The DSM-III-R categorical personality disorder diagnoses: A critique and an alternative". *Psychological Inquiry*. **4** (2): 75–90. doi:10.1207/s15327965pli0402_1.

Costa, P.T., & Widiger, T.A. (2001). Personality disorders and the five-factor model of personality (2nd ed.). Washington, DC: American Psychological Association.

Samuel, D.B.; Widiger, T.A. (2008). "A meta-analytic review of the relationships between the five-factor model and DSM personality disorders: A facet level analysis". *Clinical Psychology Review*. **28** (8): 1326–42.:10.1016/j.cpr.2008.07.002. PMC 2614445. PMID 18708274.

Widiger, Thomas A., Costa, Paul T. (2012). Personality Disorders and the Five-Factor Model of Personality, Third Edition. ISBN 978-1-4338-1166-1.

Young, M.D., Deardorff, J., Ozer, E., & Lahiff, M. (2011) Sexual abuse in childhood and adolescence and the risk of early pregnancy among women ages 18-22. *Journal of Adolescent Health, 49*, 287-293.